Veterans with PTSD Hope with Oils Project

Essential Oils Companion Book

Look Us Up on Facebook

Disclaimer

No part of this publication may be reproduced or transmitted in any form or by any means, mechanical or electronic, including photocopying or recording, or by any information storage and retrieval system, or transmitted by email without permission in writing from the publisher.

All brand names, whether implied or inferred used in this book are trademarked names of their respective holders. We are not associated with any product in this book. This writing in whole or in part is the opinion of the authors only and does not express opinions of any company.

While all attempts and efforts have been made to verify the information held within this publication, neither the author nor the publisher assumes any responsibility for errors, omissions, or opposing interpretations of the content herein.

This book is for entertainment purposes only. The views expressed are those of the author alone, and should not be taken as expert instruction or commands. The reader of this book is responsible for his or her own actions when it comes to reading the book.

Adherence to all applicable laws and regulations, including international, federal, state, and local governing professional licensing, business practices, advertising, and all other aspects of doing business in the US, Canada, or an other jurisdiction is the sole responsibility of the purchaser or reader.

Neither the author nor the publisher assumes any responsibility or liability whatsoever on the behalf of the purchaser or reader of these materials.

Any received slight of any individual or organization is purely unintentional.

Revised Edition

Published in the United States by: Oils4Warriors

Printed in the United States
Cover and Text Design: Susan Leslie
Content: Oils4Warriors

Unless otherwise noted, photos are royalty free courtesy of Google images

ISBN-13:978-0692609460 (GodsOils)
ISBN-10:0692609466

Table of Contents

This writing is dedicated to my daughter,

and
all warriors

who made it home,

but left their souls and friends behind
on fields of conflict across oceans.

Yours is another battle at the home front.

****

Introduction & Dedication

The intention here with writing a Warriors Hope with Oils book, is to offer help with application, methods, and techniques. It is not my intention to describe every detail of trauma and shock from being in a battle zone, because if you are reading this, you already have some idea what you're dealing with....OR you have already ordered every book on the subject and are still searching for answers. I know your desperation has led you to read this. I am very "low-tech" in this writing and that is intentional. I am not a doctor or psychologist. I just know what has worked for our family, and that is OILS. I am not going to describe in scientific detail how oils work in the body; because you just need them to work, right? If you want to know more, see the book reference list in the appendix. My disclaimer is I am not a counselor or doctor. I can't heal you. Nobody but G-d can heal, and our body systems were intelligently designed to heal on their own when given what they need.

In some cases, doctors are needed, and you must make that determination on your own. (The statements in this book have not been evaluated by the FDA and cannot diagnose, cure, prevent. prescribe or treat anyone. Professional medical attention is always advised)

Largely, we have discovered oils that work by just using them and experimenting. I hope this saves you some grief and gives you a shortcut in using the oils for supporting calmness, restful sleep, healthy breathing, helping detoxification of the body, and balancing body systems in general; "restoring homeostasis" as they say. For anyone who has been through trauma, it's not a matter of "getting back to normal" but "finding your new normal". Oils will greatly support your journey to find this!

There are many plant extracts that offer relief of imbalances in the body systems. Take for example medical marijuana, which I am all in favor of, if it helps. Problem is, not everyone chooses medical marijuana. Some people feel that medical marijuana is cost prohibitive and hard to acquire, with a lot of social stigma to go along with it. For those with breathing issues, medical marijuana is out of the question as far as smoking it. To us, therapeutic grade essential oils have provided an excellent alternative in taking control of one's healthcare! You don't need a prescription to use the oils, and they are very effective in restoring natural balance in body systems.

It seems in this life, that we struggle in finding what we need at times. It's like no matter where we turn we hit a brick wall; that our efforts are futile. A lot of times, we don't know the right questions to ask. Much of life is knowing what questions to be asking in any situation. As soon as we ask, the answers start appearing. Many times we don't know the right questions, because we keep asking the same questions expecting different answers....life just does not work that way. You have to flow with life. ♠

What we've learned. In fact, beating down the doors of Congressmen and professionals in that system, made us frustrated and upset a lot. It did not help that a lot of Veterans seem to get everything they need. But, that just was not happening for our family. I knew in my heart, there had to be others out there who had slipped through the cracks. I thought, since we had found something that had made life more tolerable for my daughter, it might help others.

I hope you will find some relief using oils, as we and many others have. The oils that we have experience with and can attest to are a certain brand of oils. I cannot speak for how other brands work, as we are stating what worked for us. We have no desire to try other brands of oils. This company has a consistent standard that we have come to count on for our health.

Again, always seek professional medical care.

One Starfish

It's a warm summer day in June, 2003.

An Army vehicle has just arrived in your driveway.

Your daughter is deployed in a war zone.

Your knees buckle, and you feel faint.

You know they will knock on the door.....you peek around the corner. You figure if they don't see you, they can't give you any bad news. It won't be real if you just stay out of sight.

Someone emerges from the driver's side. He has a pleasant look on his face. Another person emerges from the passenger side, a woman, and she is smiling. You ask yourself, "why are they smiling?"

They approach the door. You know you must respond.

With heart racing, you prepare for the news: your child is coming home in a coffin.

But it's not that! They say your child is alive! You drop to your knees in gratitude. You spontaneously burst into tears of joy! Anything is workable now! You can handle ANYTHING as long as your beloved child is alive, you reassure yourself.

Little did we know how unprepared we were for such a calamity.

I cannot tell you because we have lost count, and it would take hundreds of pages to express how many thousands of times that bomb has exploded since then. It has exploded in our minds, our imaginations, our flashbacks, our family, our finances, our journey. We have never known "where" that "bomb" will explode next.....perhaps we never will. But, now we can honestly say, that after nine years of Veterans Administration craziness trying and failing to get my daughter's needs met, we have a coping tool, until more help arrives. This coping tool did not come from the mind of big government, but the mind of Creation itself, in plant-form and has been used for thousands of years....this is "why" we personally use essential oils for war trauma effects.

My daughter was hurt very badly with multiple injuries after an anti-tank landmine exploded the truck she was a co-driver of. Her ranking officer and driver of the massive PLS (palletized Load System) truck, managed to prevent it from overturning after the explosion, and, after freeing himself, pulled her from the wreckage, essentially saving her life.

Immediately after the accident, her strapping twenty year-old boyfriend who had insisted on joining the National Guard with her to "watch her back", rushed to her side and held her body in a certain fixed position for more than eight hours, virtually turning himself into a "human traction device" at the field hospital before she could be safely evacuated to the Landstuhl Regional Medical hospital in Germany.

Her spine was fractured and she suffered a Traumatic Brain Injury(TBI) when the force of the explosion slammed her head into the top of the cab. The explosion had sent metal shards deep into her 115 lb frame, and the scorching metal stung her frail body like a hot knife when it penetrated her knees, back and arms. When her sister and I had seen her last, she was a vibrant girl of twenty, full of life, and loving the Army life....now we were picking up a shell of what she once was; the remnants of her soul, body and mind that was vaporized over the sands of Iraq, forever beckoning to her from the distant land.

It's a struggle to know how to tell this story with the attention it deserves, but suffice it to say, that with it being such a huge subject for so many, I can only tell our little part of it. We are "one starfish"... like the story of the man, who was walking along the beach, when he noticed a boy ahead of him, bending down and picking up, one at a time, stranded starfish that had been left when the tide went out. Then he would gently toss each one back into the sea. The man was intrigued, and he caught up to the boy and asked him, "Why are you throwing the starfish into the sea? What does it matter? You cannot possibly save all the starfish!" And the boy replied, " it does too matter!....it matters to the one starfish"!

Our family, and perhaps your family, is the "one starfish". It is our belief that each of us can help one starfish....one veteran at a time. Can our "why" be your "why"?

The Situation: War is Hell at Home

After my daughter returned from Iraq, she started purchasing fragrant oils in roller bottles on the internet from the Middle East and India. I never paid much attention to this, I thought they were just perfumes. We realize now, of course, her body and mind were intuitively craving natural oils.

We were thrust into an unknown abyss of desolation. We did not know where to turn. A lot of our efforts were dead-ends, consumed with doctor appointments, back injury, and a plethora of injuries that seemed completely overwhelming. There were people pinning medals on her, debriefing her on what she could say and couldn't say to the press, who were constantly calling for interviews.

The doctors prescribed pills. I was packing deep shrapnel wounds on her body two times a day; a process of stuffing cotton wadding deep into the holes in her body from the blast, so that it would heal from the bottom up, and listening to the wails of pain and grief. She kept saying over and over, “I need to get back to my unit! I need to go back to Iraq!”

We spent many a day at a Veteran's Hospital together, only to wind up at the pharmacy with another pain med prescription or anti-depressant script. My daughter did not want to get hooked on pain medication and did not want to take pills....she wanted real answers to her health problem.

The hospital staff did not address any of her problems regarding plastic surgery she needed, or chiropractic treatments she could use, as we watched her spine curve a little more with each passing year. They didn't help at all with the shrapnel issue, or the fact that her right leg is completely unusable half the time, or the fact that she was having seizures. The veterans administrative personnel added to the problems, by telling her to “get her affairs in order”over the phone.

All the letters I had written to Congressmen on her behalf didn't do a thing. They passed the buck every time. It was so frustrating and exhausting, Where were all the people who pinned medals on her when she came home? Where were they?

Just when things couldn't get any worse, including the fact that she was financially destitute, 100% disabled, and not receiving proper compensation (and still isn't to this day), she awoke one day with TERROR....PTSD had set in. She had somehow warded it off for three years; she had never “believed” in it. She always felt that “it was all in a soldiers' head.” Now suddenly, it was as if she was reliving the explosion, and was AT the event again....Terror gripped her, her whole body went into stiffness, she screamed. Her eyes would be open, but she couldn't see me. It was as if she was in Iraq!

We would take her to the local hospital emergency room for an injection of something to calm her. I knew she was reliving the event in a whole new way. It was so heart-wrenching. I cannot describe the desperation and helplessness we felt for many years, watching her live in hell on Earth year in, year out. I was totally unprepared for this; this was unlike anything I had ever witnessed or experienced.

Our wee family felt so desperate and out-of-control, like we were sliding down a deep hole, and we could not grip the sides to save ourselves. Every day was spent dreading a death call or a suicide call. The person dealing with the most hell of it, was of course, my daughter. I felt so sorry for her. I felt sorry for myself. I blamed myself for all of it somehow. I blamed myself for not being able to help her. The mental hell appeared to have no end for any of us.

The Beginning of Oils

In 2012, our world was still, metaphorically, at Ground Zero. My daughter's distrust of the Veteran's Administration deepened. Life was not fun. But a major shift was about to happen; I was invited to my first essential oils class. I went to it to be supportive of a friend of mine. I thought it was going to be like a candle party where you pick out differently scented products.

As the evening progressed, I learned that this class was ANYTHING BUT a candle party, and I was enlightened along with several other people about the power of essential oils. Snuggled into my friend's home with fifteen other people, I felt my brain and heart expanding as the leader taught the class. I noticed my mouth was gaping. I had never heard anything so provocative as what was being shared about these powerful molecules called essential oils. I began to write down all the questions I would be asking my former husband, a physician, on the medical side of these oils.

As the oils were passed around the room, I was enchanted with the rich, full aromas of ***Peppermint, Orange,*** and ***Lemon.*** It took me back to a day in 2004 with my daughter.

She called me to say that she had just received back her duffel bag from Iraq in a army transport of left-behind items. It had been in Iraq for a year, after the explosion. She was picking it up at the base and coming over to open it with me. She knew it would be emotional and she wanted me there. I prepared myself for the worst.

I went out to her car to meet her when she pulled up in the driveway. She unlocked the trunk and there was her bag. We both gazed at it for a moment, as if it was a silent witness and messenger of events on the other side of the world; as if it may explode.... I braced myself...

She reached into it to open it, and pulled out a wad of clothes, wrapped her slender arms around it, and pressed it into her chest and BURIED her face into the clothing. I was surprised. She looked at me and smiled and offered the pile of old clothes stained with blood and plasma....she purred, "Mom, smell this, it smells like Iraq!"

I could hardly believe she wanted me to smell that yucky mob of dirty clothes! Could she be saying she adored the smell of war and death? Really? She extended the pile to me that was spilling over in her arms, and I obliged her, burying my face in complete faith into them, too....I will never forget the fragrance, the indescribable fragrance of spice, it was fresh, the mix of roses and cinnamon, and oranges together with a hint of sea air. I was speechless. Is this what Iraq smelled like?

Together we sniffed and cried and smiled. Finally, a tiny bright spot had shone on us.

I was utterly taken aback. Army laundry never smelled so good! It was as if she got a piece of her blown up life back.

Just like I was stunned at this evening class, as the oils were being passed around, we inhaled deeply. Life would be taking a turn for the better that night.

Oils: Our Gift from the Earth

I bought an oils kit as soon as I could afford it. However, I was very, very skeptical of these oils. I had no previous experience with them, other than the store-bought lavender and tea tree oil I bought for my horses. Basically, I had no idea about what to do with them, or how to use them effectively.

I purchased a kit for my daughter to try, in faith, because we were desperate to find something for her. She was miles ahead of me, however, as she had been craving oils since she first returned from Iraq. The oils she had purchased online smelled nice, but that's about the extent of it. They were made somewhere in India and we had no clue as to the purity or potency of those oils.

At any rate, she immediately began using them, intuitively, and got immediate relief. She called me many times to say how grateful she was to my firend and me for introducing them to her.

Over time, I, too, eventually got the hang of using them. I learned the secret of essential oils! Over the next twelve months, my health began to improve significantly. My oilamony was that every year in September I would start getting colds that would turn into bronchitis, and then hang on all through winter until May. Now, since using oils and great supplements from the same company, I have health all year long!

My daughter was doing better than ever. She was regaining hope for living again! I was trying to keep her supplied with oils that she needed. Amazing things started gradually happening: she was calling with some good news occasionally. She was more mobile. She was more optimistic. She would invite me over sometimes (prior to oils she had sever agoraphobia), her sleep was improving, and suicidal thoughts were waning.

I started to imagine that maybe our relationship could be restored from the chasm that had occurred due to the complexity of PTSD and our mutual lack of tools to cope with it. One of the many reasons our relationship had been strained for years was because my conversing always turned to inquiring about her health, and she was frustrated with being mothered all the time. She just wanted to find her “new normal” and get on with being young and lively, and pick up where she left off.

She was plagued with terror and fear in lots of daily activities. She had trouble driving because if she saw anything ahead of the car like a piece of garbage, or anything remotely looking like a foreign object that could explode, she would be triggered into an episode. Also, her physical frame had been taxed beyond limit, not to mention the emotional toll that she had to bear.

But now, we were having a reprieve! The oils were providing a huge distraction from the normal maelstrom of pain and anguish we endured. There were days of peace now. Emergency room visits were less frequent. Things were/are noticeably improved.

Housekeeping: Before you start using oils

Just a few 'housekeeping' things to go over before you get started with using the oils:

☻ Our experience and testimonials in this book are with a specific type of Essential Oils batch-tested for purity. Quality of oils varies from company to company. Always dilute them in 2:1 ratio: two drops carrier oil with one drop essential oil. Sometimes they can go on NEAT (without dilution) but we recommend dilution as these oils are very strong. The most effective oils routine is pre-emptive use of oils and products to support the body. Oils are easily incorporated into any therapy setting or medical routine upon approval from your physician or therapist, and enhance life's journey tremendously.

☻ Dilute essential oils if they get into the eyes. Batch-tested for purity, essential oils will not harm the eyes, but it can be very uncomfortable. Use one drop of carrier oil to one drop essential oil as needed into the eye. DO NOT USE WATER TO WASH OUT ESSENTIAL OIL as it will only drive the oil further into eye, and take longer to dissipate. Do not use any of the citrus oils in plastic containers, as the natural acids will eat through the plastic.

☻ Batch-tested for purity essential oils are to be used TOPICALLY, AROMATICALLY, and INTERNALLY:

▪*Aromatically diffusing oils*: use only diffusers designated for use with oils to achieve maximum benefits without damaging the oils' therapeutic benefits. They can also be inhaled straight from the bottle. Get three or four diffusers for your home when possible.

▪ *Internally using oils:* use pure veggie caps to put drops of oil into to take orally. Dilution is suggested.

Also can be added to drinking water, or even to a shot glass.

▪*Topical use:* on skin, but care is used for skin sensitivity through dilution; also used in baths.

Key Reflex points on body: head, face, ears, shoulders, wrists, navel, inner thighs, abdomen, spine, bottoms of feet.

☮Caution is used for hotter oils, such as *Oregano, Cinnamon, Deep Blue drops*; DILUTE 1:1

☮Caution: If using Citrus oils topically, do not expose yourself to sunlight on that part of the body for at least 12 hours!! Severe sunburn can occur.

Benefits of Oil Use:

- ☯ Essential oils assist physically
- ☯ Essential oils assist in the heart
- ☯ Essential oils assist in changing old beliefs
- ☯ Essential oils assist spiritually
- ☯ Essential oils inspire life's true purpose

☻ Always respect the oils. They are strong compounds, not to be underestimated. Start with one drop and work your way up if it's well-tolerated. Think of oils as super-concentrated, non-caloric food drops!

CHAPTER 1

☼ Start of the Day Ritual ☼

(no matter when it is, morning, night, wee hours)

Not enough emphasis can be put on the fact that routine gives results. Sometime in your 24 hour day, there must be a foundation laid for improving the health on a regular basis. Start with resolve leading to the decision to at least try for 30 days what is suggested in this book.

- Put three oils by your bedside, in a nice small basket or something; we call them "The FLiP Trinity" - ***Frankincense, Lavender,*** and ***Peppermint***. Have them available at all times during the sleep cycle you have. When you wake up in the night, from nightmares or shock, use ***Peppermint*** immediately to shift the brain. It cools your head down and brings you out. Put a drop on your finger and rub on top of forehead and temples. It will take about 30 seconds. Also, use your favorite soul support oils.
- Another good one is the ***Lavender,***or ***Calming Blend***. Massage it around your outer ears when awakened.
- ***Frankincense*** goes under the tongue, 2 drops before rising. It tastes kind of bad, but you will grow to appreciate it.
- Keep ***Respiratory DROPS*** near your bed, too. You can suck on one while going back to sleep.
- When you get out of bed to do your thing, have ready your enzymes and your probiotics to take before eating anything, if possible. Especially the probiotics because they help so much with emotional imbalances and strengthening GUT health and immunity!

The supplements are very, very important for laying the foundation of restored balance because they are in a matrix that anyone's body can absorb efficiently. They are utilized by the body efficiently. They are not like store-bought vitamins where a lot of them end up in the crapper.

- ➢ Take the full dose of 2 of each of vitamin at start of day, and 2 of each 4 hours before bedtime. You will notice improved energy, and improved sleep. Do this for 30 days. If the vitamins don't work (but they will) or if you don't like them for any reason, return the empty bottles for a full refund (only after 30 day period.
- ➢ Two hours after waking, use another drop of ***Frankincense*** under the tongue. Pre-emptive use is a better approach with oils. They are way better acting when you apply them every 2-3 hours.

Use another ***Respiratory Drop with Melissa*** in it if needed. Experience and trial and error are the best ways to learn for yourself.

ESSENTIAL OIL OMEGA COMPLEX

(vitamin supplement)

• Promotes healthy cardiovascular, nervous, and immune system function. • Supports healthy joint function and comfort • Provides important modulating nutrients for healthy immune function • Protects against lipid oxidation and supports healthy function of the brain • Promotes healthy skin • Both marine and plant-sourced omega oils from sustainable sources

► Suggested use: 2 softgels orally, at start of day, 2 softgels about 3 hours before going to sleep.

FOOD NUTRIENT COMPLEX (vitamin supplement)

• Provides 22 essential vitamins and minerals to support normal growth, function, and maintenance of cells • Fights free radicals with the antioxidant vitamins A, C, and E • Supports healthy metabolism and cellular energy • Supports bone health with calcium, magnesium, zinc, and vitamin D • Supports healthy immune function • Supports healthy digestion • Provides systemic benefits of vitality and wellness associated with optimal intake of essential nutrients • Provides a balanced blend of essential antioxidant vitamins A, C, and E, an energy complex of B vitamins, and 800 IU of vitamin D • Delivers a unique blend of health-promoting polyphenols from a variety of healthy fruits and vegetables, including resveratrol, grape, citrus and pomegranate • Includes a balanced blend of minerals including calcium, magnesium, zinc, selenium, copper, manganese, chromium, and other chelated minerals • Contains natural vitamin E tocopherols and tocotrienols • Includes proprietary digestive blend of ***Peppermint, Ginger,*** and Caraway Seed • Made with sodium lauryl sulfate-free vegetable capsules.

► Suggested use 2 capsules after rising and eating breakfast, and 2 capsules three hours before bed.

PROBIOTIC DEFENSE FORMULA

(live 'good' bacteria for small intestine)

• Supports healthy digestive functions and immunities while creating an unfavorable environment for unhealthy elements • Helps boost GI immunities

Special double-encapsulation protects flora from stomach acid as they pass through.

► Take two mid-morning to support physical and emotional health.

By the time you get done taking all these vitamins, it's time to take some more!! But just do it! It really helps!!

ENZYME SUPPORT

• Supports healthy digestion and metabolism of enzyme-deficient, processed foods • Speeds conversion of food nutrients to cellular energy • Promotes gastrointestinal comfort and food tolerance • Supports healthy production of metabolic enzymes

► Take two capsules before first meal of the day

This is a comparison. Notice swelling and inflammation at shrapnel scarring on knees.

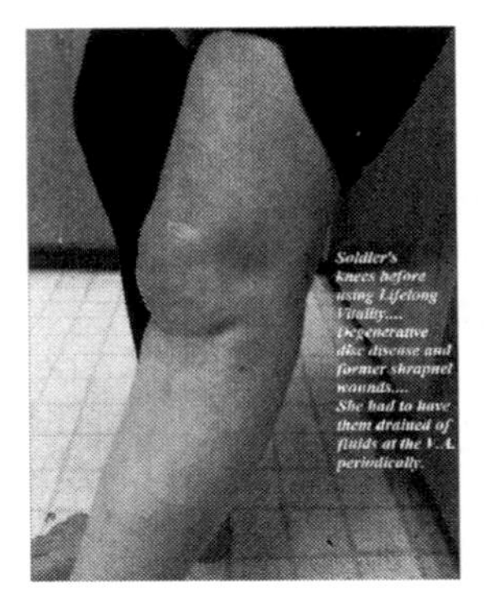

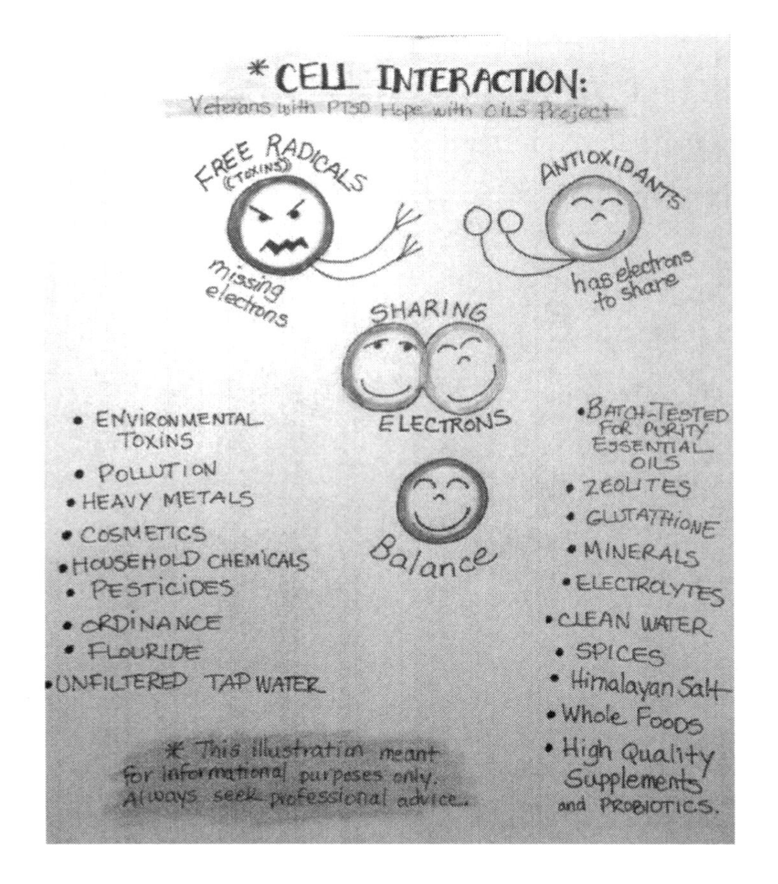

CHAPTER 2

How to Curb Anger~Worry~Fear~ Anxiousness

There is nothing more damaging to ourselves and others we love, as a fit of rage or to be in a frequent state of anger, which stems from fear, and leads to either a feeling of being out-of-control or trying to control everything. Being fearful is crushing to the immunity of the body and rips proverbial holes into our souls. Everything and anything should be attempted to curb rage and its effects on relationships.

If we are honest with ourselves, we know that a sincere attempt at additional emotional work will be in order and essential oils will support that. Hopefully, Warriors will reach out to another combat vet and talk. This begins the recovery process. Use oils to help bring about courage to do this work. Use oils for calming and relaxation at a cellular level. Trust the oils. Give them an honest 30 day trial of consistency and you will be amazed.

Melissa & Respiratory Drops, Peppermint, Calming Blend, Frankincense, Geranium, Ylang Ylang, Women's Monthly Blend

Anxious Feelings ~ ***Bergamot, Melissa, Encouraging Blend*** (contains ***Melissa), Reassuring Blend, Renewing Blend, Basil, Respiratory Blend, Tension Blend***

Fear ~ ***Reassuring Blend, Inspiring Blend, Vetiver, Cinnamon, Birch, Cassia, Cypress, Lavender, Myrrh***

In addition to your oils at home, there are two tools that will really help in your efforts with curbing angry feelings: a good essential oils *diffuser* and an oils *keychain* for having the oils at-the-ready on outings. Any sincere effort of oils requires them being available <u>*AND*</u> a commitment to using them every two hours. I know, it seems like a lot, but isn't it worth trying for yourself and your loved ones?

The ***diffuser*** pictured here is called the **<u>Aroma Ace Diffuser.</u>** It's like a hospital-grade one. It diffuses PURE oil, no water mixed in. This is the diffuser for occasional depression and cleansing the home. Run it as often as you can, 24/7 in occupied rooms with a citrus oil attached, or preferably, ***Joyful Blend*** or ***Invigorating Blend,*** or your favorite of the Soul Support Collection of oils. But if you are on a strict budget, ***Lemon*** or ***Orange*** will definitely help. This particular diffuser requires cleaning only once a year, and is what we call a "workhorse".

A diffuser helps occasional agitated or anxious feelings throughout the day and night. Many of you are unable to sleep or get on a regular schedule. That's okay. Trust the oils and give them an honest 30 day try. Run your diffuser as often as possible.

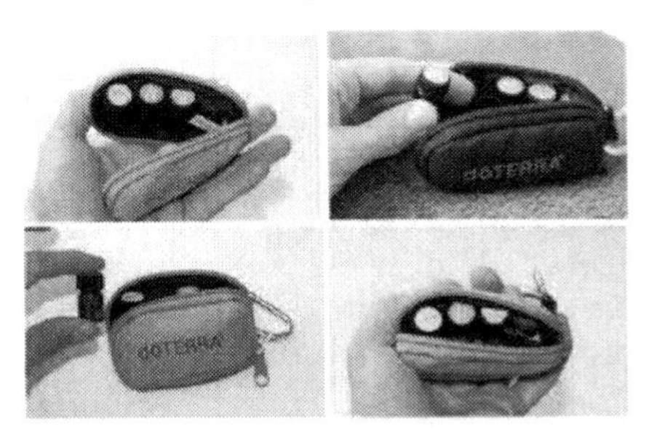

The ***keychain*** concept is for quick availability of oils application away from home. This is important for alleviating indications of an on-coming "event". If you want to carry full 15ml bottles with you, that's okay, too. The keychain requires refilling sometimes as often as daily, but offers a more discrete container. But then again, who cares if it's working!

Melissa or Black Pepper ~ Diffuse this oil or inhale. Also can be applied with little or no dilution. This is a plant that can be easily grown in your garden or a pot. I have grown it and it's very low maintenance. Keep in mind the oil is super concentrated and you will need a LOT of the plant to equal one drop of ***Melissa*** oil.

► ***Respiratory Drops*** contain ***Melissa***, and are super~effective for calming! And they are easy to slip into your purse or pocket.

► ***Joyful Blend*** also contains ***Melissa*** oil. Diffuse it liberally for angriness and frustration. Apply 2 drops to brain stem as needed for agitated and anxious feelings.

►The pure oil is suggested, however, for maximum benefits. Try to obtain the purest ***Melissa*** oil you can.

►Apply one drop to bottom of each foot as needed. The feet absorb oils very quickly and efficiently.

Peppermint ~ is part of a "Holy Trinity" of oils. There seems to be some "magic" to this combination in helping support the body.

Peppermint has a super~cooling effect for head discomfort; apply preemptively at onset of rage and after rage. It is very strong. One drop = 28 cups of Peppermint tea, so start with one drop! Try it! My daughter can't live without it.

►Use one drop on upper forehead for headache, rub in, dilute for sensitive skin types. Also, rub on back of neck. Combine with ***Frankincense*** for super invigorating effect.

Respiratory Drops ~Very calming for occasional anxious feelings. They contain ***Melissa***, too, which is very calming.

►Use one ***Respiratory Drop*** for calming, or brew a mug of your favorite tea and place one drop into the hot tea! It's very soothing to the system. Listen to the crackle in the mug as it melts to release all the goodness.

Calming Blend ~ For those who don't care for the strong scent of straight ***Lavender*** by itself, ***Calming Blend*** is the blend to try. It has a mellower aroma to it. Many people suffering from Post-War stuff love this oil for promoting sleep and calm feelings. Blends provide a great way to try oils when you are first starting out because you are not buying them each individually. But, as you become more in-tune with the oils and more skilled at listening to your body, you will want to buy them individually, too.

►Inhale straight from bottle during onset of stress. Diffuse in occupied areas.

►Massage two drops on bottom of each foot at bedtime and cover with cotton sock. Also, you may want to diffuse at bedtime. Try one or the other first, and do more if needed. Can also be applied straight on filter of CPAP machine.

►Can be worn as perfume or cologne. Mix with ***White Fir*** for masculine scent. See R.I.P blend recipe.

Frankincense ~ Part of the Trinity of Oils, this oil is essential for brain-shock, brain balance.

►Put 1-2 drops under tongue. Also massage on brain stem. Inhale for relaxation.

►Use 2 drops under tongue before rising out of bed. Use another 2 drops after 3:00 pm. You may want to use more if needed. It's very hard to have too much, but because of expense, just start with this.

►Apply one drop on scarred areas of skin. Use 1-2 times a day

►Inhale from bottle during emotional work when you want to have more clarity. Or diffuse in diffuser.

►Combine one drop ***Frankincense*** and one drop ***Peppermint*** on hand, rub together, cup over nose and inhale for super clarity and focus. Best to do at "lull" times of day, like at work after you eat lunch.

►Use daily for best results!!

Geranium ~

►Use by itself or with ***Frankincense*** when doing emotional breathing work. Put one drop of each in hands, rub together and cup over nose to inhale. Rub on brain stem.

►Massage 1 drop on bottom of each foot. Inhale from bottle, or diffuse in occupied areas.

►Apply one drop on each wrist for relaxation.

► Anxiety Inhalant: Put 2 drops ***Geranium***, 2 drops ***Ylang Ylang***, 3 drops ***Frankincense***, 1 drop ***Vetiver*** on hands. Rub together, cup over nose and inhale.

►***Geranium*** Tea: A few drops in honey or agave then add hot water (not boiling) to soothe occasional loose stools due to travel.

►Use one drop on washrag with your regular soap for facial wash or body wash. Make sure you do the skin test on inside of elbow to check for sensitivity.

Ylang-Ylang ~

►Gently massage over heart, or have partner massage in. Can be used during a massage on ears before intimacy.

►Inhale deeply during times of stress and agitation.

Women's Monthly Blend ~ Don't ya just hate it when someone points out that your irritability could be "your time of the month"? And this gets used as a blame tactic? Well, rest assured, this blend will work if it is, or if it isn't! ☺ and it is often mistaken for fine perfume! It comes in a purse-size 10 oz. roller bottle making it easy to apply whenever and wherever. Great for hot-flashes too.

►Roll it on during or after flashbacks.

►Apply to chest, abdomen, or back of neck as needed.

►Diffuse in occupied areas.

***"He who has health, has hope;
and he who has hope,
has everything."***

-Thomas Carlyle

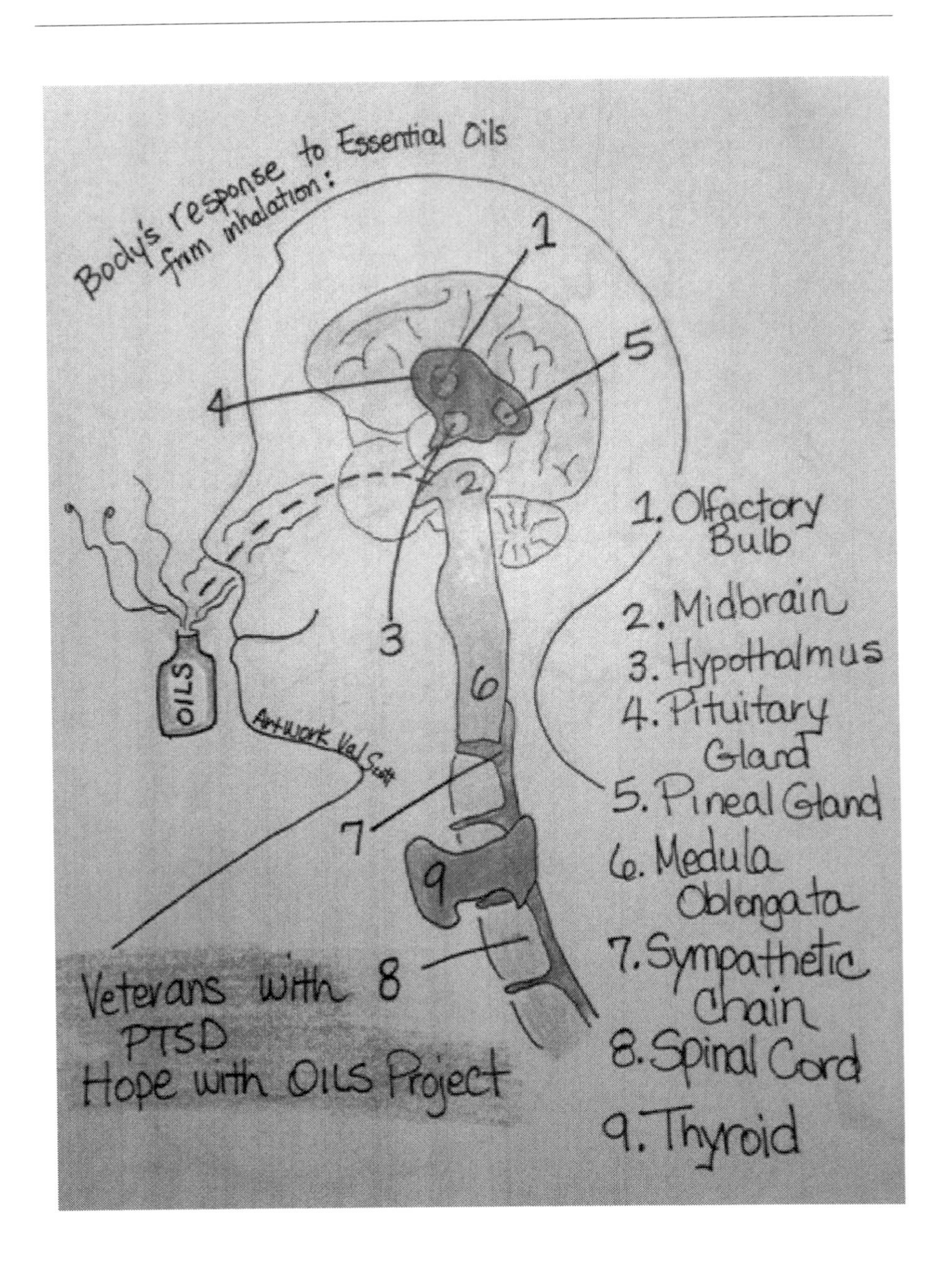
Body's response to Essential Oils from inhalation:
1
2
3
4
5
6
7
8
9
OILS
ArtWork Val Scott
1. Olfactory Bulb
2. Midbrain
3. Hypothalmus
4. Pituitary Gland
5. Pineal Gland
6. Medula Oblongata
7. Sympathetic Chain
8. Spinal Cord
9. Thyroid
Veterans with PTSD
Hope with OILS Project

CHAPTER 3

How to Use a Massage Table to Help Soldier Families

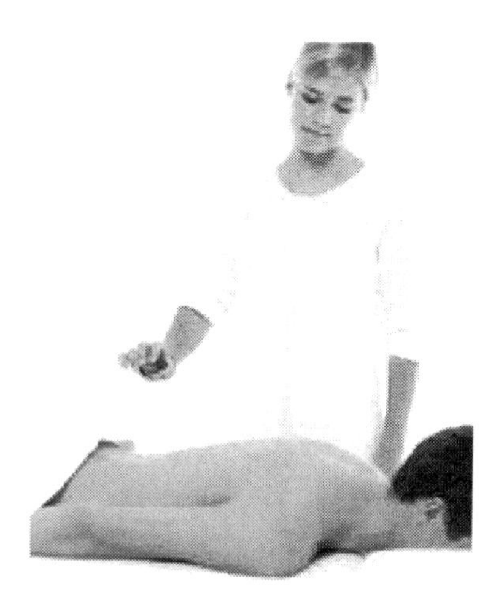

Using a massage table and implementing some easy relaxation techniques using essential oils, you will find benefits for both the giver and receiver. It can really help with supporting overall bodily health and relaxation, as well as bring back *homeostasis* to a taxed body and mind! In this ever-increasing stressful culture we find ourselves in, we must take the time to take care of our health. Receiving a relaxation technique is a great tool and should be done on a regular basis.

Homeostasis is a fancy word for balance. It addresses different stressors in the body, at a cellular level, by applying oils with touching techniques on the back (spine), hands, and feet. Exposure to an array of toxins in the world today weakens the immune system and creates imbalances in the body.

It is well documented in modern science that visceral points and whole system energy meridians exist (duh, it's been in Chinese medicine for centuries!) and that the energy contact points are the hands, feet, and ears. It is a restorative to do one of these on someone after intense episodes of discomfort that have racked the body. You can also perform one on someone who is in the hospital! Just have them roll on their side or give you their hands and feet to work on. We hear of a father whose son was in an accident and had paralysis. The father knew about the techniques and sought out someone who knew how to do it. He was shown how to do it for his son while he lay in his hospital bed. The son began recovering quickly.

I will tell you a trade secret;

all healing is self-healing.

~ Dr. Albert Schwietzer

The limbic system is thought to be the seat of our emotions. When aroma has been detected, cognitive recognition occurs only after it has been relayed to the brain cortex. By the time we correctly identify the aroma its scent has long since activated deep-seated emotional responses through the limbic system. ** EXAMPLE: smelling Grandmas cookies baking! Or, the smell of sulphur or metal exploding triggering an episode. (Use Eucalyptus to shift this.) A simple internet search using "oils technique on massage table' will pull up some ways to learn about palm slides, thumb walks, chakras, ear massage, foot massage, etc.

A relaxation technique with oils is FREE OF CHARGE, unless it's performed by a LMT (Licensed Massage Therapist) when there may be applicable charges. It was developed as a tool for families to use because of the often stressful existence we live in this world. It is a de-stressor tool. It can also be used as a reliever of toxic emotions.

The first time I gave my daughter a relaxation technique, she got huge benefit from it. I was a little surprised how much benefit she got, as she began sobbing with her face down in the cheek cradle. It was a solemn moment for sure. She was out of pain for about eight hours, which brought on a different sort of event known as euphoric anxiety. This is when the pain that has grounded someone in their body, suddenly leaves. It is a feeling of not knowing if you have died and left your body. As she became more comfortable with not being in pain, she said she wanted to stay up that night and enjoy the feeling! She moved around a lot the rest of the evening, as if to test" this new sensation for the next few hours, commenting to me about how cool it was to be completely out of pain. ♥

The oils used in order are:

- ***Grounding Blend***~spruce, rosewood, blue tansy, frankincense, fractionated coconut oil.*
- ***Lavender***~pure
- ***Melaleuca***~pure
- ***Protective Blend***~ a blend of orange, clove, cinnamon, eucalyptus, rosemary
- ***Massage Blend***~a blend of cypress, marjoram, basil, lavender, grapefruit, peppermint
- ***Deep Soothing Blend***~a blend of wintergreen, camphor, peppermint, blue tansy, blue chamomile, helichrysum, osmanthus
- ***Orange***~pure
- ***Peppermint***~pure

The compounds and constituents found in EACH one of these oils, are health-enhancing all on their own, let alone being layered in a 40 minute session like this. You feel great after one of these! Sometimes people say how they could finally take a huge bowel movement afterwards (☺), some people take a nap afterwards, and some just relax the rest of the day after receiving one...But be aware that the feelings of each individual are unique to them, and no one can anticipate exactly how you will benefit the most. Try it and see! What have you got to lose? It's FREE! Maybe your spouse or partner will want to learn the technique by attending a Certification class so they can give you the suggested two relaxation techniques a week.

There is also the option of just doing hands and feet if a massage table is not accessible.

►Search the Battle Buddy List of Advocates to see if someone near you knows how to give a relaxation technique. The Battle Buddy List can be found on our Facebook page: Veterans with PTSD Hope with Oils Project, under "more" dropdown menu, then notes. It depends on what device you are viewing it from as to where the 'notes' are found. It sometimes appears in the lefthand side pane. ☺

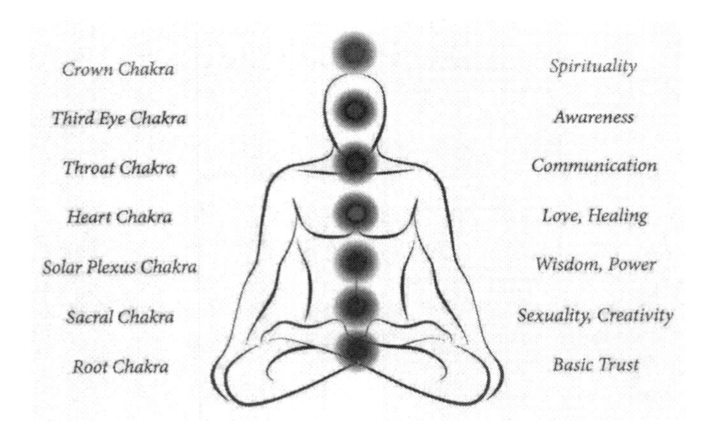

CHAPTER 4

Self-Medicating Alternatives

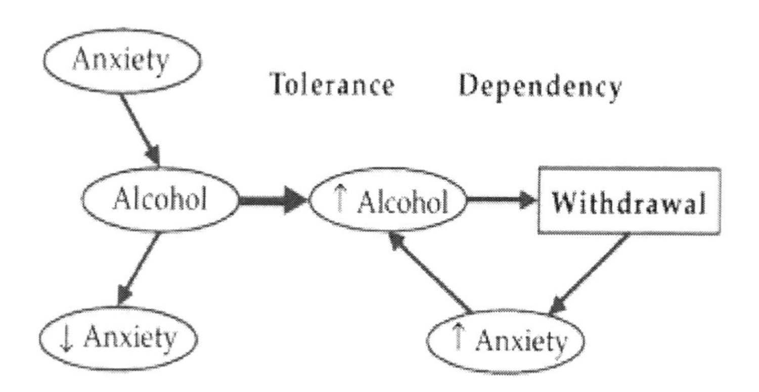

Cravings & Dependence

Dependence is very common in warriors as a result of self-medicating to survive. We do not judge this good or bad; it's a survival trait to keep us alive until something presents itself to take us to the next step.

With many different kinds of dependence taking place, we will make a few suggestions to help with supporting the body through the process of recovering. There is no pressure to do anything. It's entirely up to the individual to employ these suggestions for whatever they desire help with.

Note: It is suggested to drink plenty of water (with 2 drops ***lemon*** in a each 16 oz glass while detoxifying) and get enough fiber to bind toxins to help them leave the body. Also, professional medical care is always advised.

CLOVE BUD~

Steam distillation from bud and stem.

• Powerful antioxidant properties • Promotes circulation • Supports cardiovascular health • Helps soothe teeth and gums • Promotes oral health • Supports a healthy immune system • Powerful for regaining emotional strength * Numbing *

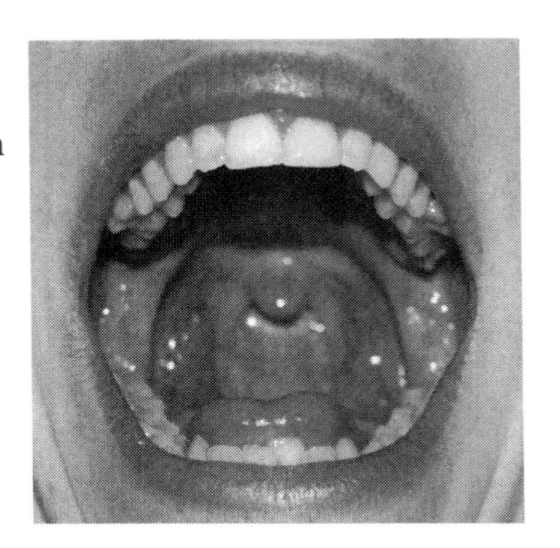

Use one drop on tip of finger and apply to roof of mouth, and back upper molars. Combine with one drop of ***Vetiver*** for super sedative effect. ***Clove*** is rather strong tasting when you first put it in mouth, but then super numbing. Can also be applied to scar tissue and shrapnel sites for numbing effect.

Companion oils: ***Vetiver, Ginger, Birch, Black Pepper, Melalueca***

TRIVIA: Essential oils are 70 times stronger than herbs. You would have to suck on about 100 clove buds to get the effect of one drop of oil.

BLACK PEPPER~

Steam distilled from berries.

Rich source of antioxidants • Supports healthy circulation *Aids digestion *Comforting and stimulating

►Use a drop under tongue before you want to light up a cigarette and see what happens! Also combine with one drop ***Clove*** for super~effect!

►You can also use this topically on tummy (combined with a drop of carrier oil for dilution) to sooth achiness or crampyness.

►Diffuse in a room while it's occupied.

Companion oils: ***Clove, Vetiver, Frankincense, Cinnamon, Lavender, Detoxification Blend***

TRIVIA: Black Pepper was considered more valuable than GOLD in ancient times for it's medicinal properties.

These statements have not been evaluated by the Food and Drug Administration. This product is not intended to diagnose, treat, cure, or prevent any disease.

Detoxification Bath Recipe

Prepare bathroom by diffusing ***Inspiring Blend***.

Add the following into running water:

- 1/2 cup baking soda
- 2 drops ***Ginger***
- 3 drops ***Frankincense***
- 1 drop ***Cypress***
- 1 drop ***Eucalyptus***

Replenish deyhdration of bathing by drinking purified water or hot tea.

"All thy garments smell of myrrh, and aloes,
and cassia, out of the ivory palaces,
whereby they have made thee glad. "
-Psalms 45:8

"Thy plants are an orchard of pomegranates, with pleasant fruits; camphor, with spikenard, Spikenard and saffron; calamus and cinnamon, with all trees of frankincense; myrrh and aloes, with all the chief spices."
Song of Solomon 4:13, 14

"....and when they had opened their treasures,
they presented unto him gifts; gold, and frankincense,
and myrrh."
-Matthew 2:11

"...and the fruit thereof shall be for meat,
and the leaf thereof for medicine."
Ezekiel 47:12

"....and the leaves of the tree were for the healing
of the nations."
Rev. 22:2

CHAPTER 5
How to Combat Depression/Apathy

The oils suggested for occasional depression due to memories are: ***Soul Support Collection of oils, Joyful Blend, Invigorating Blend, Orange, Lemon, Respiratory Blend, Lime.*** Depression and apathy can be a general feeling of 'what's the point?' Everyone is depressed from time to time, but it's not good to stay there all the time.

► Diffuse 24/7 in occupied areas and sleeping area until mood stabilizes or improves. This can take weeks, but hang in there.

► May use your favorite Soul Support Collection oil, or ***Invigorating Blend*** in diffusers.

► Drink 1 drop ***Peppermint***, 1 drop ***Orange*** in 16 oz glass 3x per day.

► Walk outside 10 minutes per day, working up to 30 minutes. Studies show this improves mood.

► If clinical depression exists, see you doctor or therapist immediately.

► Consider getting a PTSD service dog. The oils are great for animals too!

http://www.pawsforveterans.com/

► Speak to your healthcare professional about having your thyroid tested. Heavy metal exposure can interfere with good thyroid function. (see Chapter 8) It can also be affected by lack of iodine. Speak to your doctor.

►Talk to another Battle Buddy about how you are feeling and thinking. Try to continue doing grief work. If feeling numb or apathetic, inhale oils straight from the bottles. Take your favorites in your pockets. Use them often. Try using a sketch pad to scribble your feelings. Art is a great outlet for what we feel, and even just scribbling lines will begin to express what is bottled up inside.

CHAPTER 6
How to Soothe Different Types of Discomfort

Emotional Energy Centers of the Body

Emotional Energy Centers of the Body

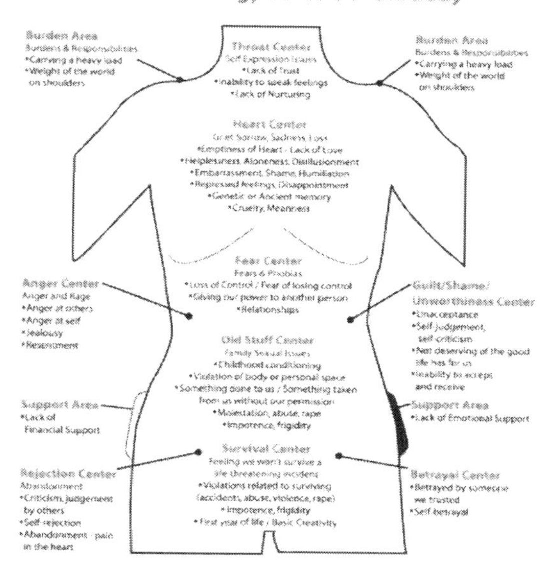

Discomfort comes in many forms. There's emotional discomfort that lodges in our tissues, there's physical discomfort from acute injury, and there's chronic (ongoing) discomfort from things like inflammation or old injuries. At any rate, there are some great oils for this.

Deep Soothing Blend, Eucalyptus, Orange, Peppermint, Lavender, Cypress, Birch, Marjoram, Basic Vitality Supplements (see Chapter 1).

Every oil has an emotional benefit as well as physical benefit.

Deep Soothing Blend comes in drops or rubbing cream, both are extremely good topically. The drops penetrate very fast, whereas the cream has a longer effect because it's in a cream form, and it has capsium (red pepper) in it.

► Apply any other suggested oil before applying ***Deep Soothing*** rubbing cream.

► Example: I worked out a bit too hard today, so I'm going to apply 1 drop ***Marjoram*** to area, then ***Deep Soothing*** cream on top.

► Apply 2 drops ***Orange*** over area then ***Deep Soothing*** cream over that if desired.

► Layer ***Marjoram*** over deep discomfort, 1-2 drops in the area, followed by 1-2 drops of ***Wintergreen*** over the top of it. ******Always seek professional medical attention for ongoing conditions. ******

Experiment with different oils to use, since each person's body chemistry is a bit unique! Soak in a tub with 10 drops of your favorite oils.

There are some great books online addressing specific oils for specific emotional needs, too. Do a Google Search.

CHAPTER 7
Groomin' with Essential Oils ~ Feelin' Good!

There are numerous essential oil products that help with looking and feeling great. We will name a few here, because my daughter wishes to express how important it is to feel pampered. She stresses the use of oils and skin care products for beauty and vitality in order to feel good and visibly improve the texture and feel of the largest organ on the body: YOUR BIRTHDAY SUIT (skin)

Internal Beauty and vitality: Use products discussed in Chapter 1 to lay a foundation of improved beauty from the inside out. Drink as much lemon oil water as possible, as this makes the skin puff up with beauty, and cleanses toxins.

Face and Hands: Get a Complete Skin Care Kit, for typical skin types, or the Skin Clearing Kit for trouble skin. These kits will last a very long time—months—and are made from essential oils and other natural products.

Wash face using cleanser from your kit. Pat dry. Proceed with Toner, then moisturizer and/or serum or anti-aging blend. You will immediately feel better and look better! Guaranteed.

****GUYS****: These products are great for you, too!! At our big Convention in Utah, I see as many or more men using the samples at the skin washing stations than women! Guys need skin care, too!

BEARD CARE

Beards need conditioning, cleansing, and care just like the hair on our heads. Even if you only have a close-trimmed beard, these recipes will keep your beard and all facial skin feeling great. Here are some ideas on making your own beard conditioning oil!

BADASS BEARD OIL BLENDS:

Step 1:

Add to a 1-oz. bottle (from Aromatools.com or other source) your preferred carrier oil of jojoba oil, sweet almond oil, fractionated coconut oil, or a little of all three using a small flask funnel, until bottle is 3/4 full. Its entirely your preference. Play with this. Each oil has a slightly different consistency. You may want to use just one of them as your base.

Jojoba oil is easily absorbed by the skin, but sort of expensive. Sweet almond oil is a bit heavier, but helps support smooth skin and prevents in-grown hairs. Coconut oil supports healthy glow, healthy microbes, and smells divine.

Step 2:

Next, add essential oils into the 1-oz. bottle of oil, a drop at a time. You want to start with 2 drops of each oil, you can always add more. Then gently shake your 1-oz bottle. Dab this mixture on fingertips and stroke into beard after shower for shine, conditioning, and natural invigorating fragrance. Make your own recipes with your favorite oils!

Babe-magnet

*1/4 oz jojoba oil
*3/4 oz sweet almond oil
*2 drops Cinnamon or Cassia oil
*2 drops Orange oil
*2 drops Melaleuca oil (tea tree)

Popeye

*3/4 oz jojoba oil
*1/4 oz sweet almond
*5 drops Melaleuca oil
*3 drops Peppermint oil

Gone in 60 Seconds

*1/2 oz jojoba oil
*1/2 oz sweet almond oil
*5 drops Peppermint oil
*2 drops Melaleuca
*2 drops Orange oil

Santa Clause

*1 oz carrier oil
*7 drops Cedarwood oil
*7 drops Sandalwood oil
*3 drops Melaleuca oil

Feet: Create your own foot-soaks, bath-soaks, and shower scrubs using bath salts, almond oils or coconut oils, and essential oils!

BATHSOAK:

3 cups Epsom salts (to soothe muscles)
2 cups sea salt
1 cup baking soda (to soften skin)
5–10 drops Serenity or Lavender essential oil (use Arborvitae or Melaleuca also if toe fungus is present)
Purple soap coloring (optional)
Mixing bowl and spoon

In a medium container with a cover: mix together Epsom salt and sea salt, breaking apart any clumps with spoon. Gradually add essential oils, mixing thoroughly. Add coloring until you've reached your desired color level. Stir in baking soda; continue mixing. Add about a cup to running water for a nice, relaxing soak.

SEE doterrablog.com or Pinterest.com for tons of DIY recipes!!

Scars: Use ***Helichrysum, Lavender, Frankincense, Geranium, Myrrh, Anti-aging Blend,*** or ***Soothing Skin Ointment*** for scarring.

► **Blend 1:** Mix 5 drops ***Helichrysum***, 5 drops ***Lavender*** with 1 Tbs. Sunflower oil or liquid lecithin and apply on location.

► **Blend 2:** Mix 1 drop ***Lavender***, 1 drop ***Geranium***; apply on location regularly.

► Use ***Comfrey Salve*** on scars.

Deodorant: Commercial deodorants and anti-perspirants contain aluminum, a neurotoxin and carcinogen. Use oils when possible. Apply 2 drops ***Grounding Blend*** or ***Melaleuca*** under each arm after skin test for sensitivity. Or use oil of your choice after skin testing.

Comfrey Salve Recipe:

In a glass Visionware cookware 5Qt, or a stainless steel cooking pot, add:

2 c. Comfrey dried leaves
1 c. Plantain dried leaves
1 c. Calendula (marigold) dried flowers and stems
1 c. Chaparrel leaf dried
1 c. Arnica flowers
3 Tbsp. Slippery Elm Powder
2 Tbsp. Goldenseal Root Powder
2 Tbsp. Propolis ("bee glue")
2 Tbsp. Myrrh Gum Powder
30 drops Vitamin E Oil
Lavender or oils of your choice (ADD LATER)
½ c.-1 c. grated beeswax or beads
Olive oil, enough to cover herbs in cooking container

Directions:

You want the oil to be gently infused with the herbs. Slowly heat everything in 125 degree oven for 3 hours until beeswax is melted.

Or, you can put container in sun for up to three days.

Next, use cheesecloth and strain mixture into a pourable container and squeeze excess out of 'herb ball'.

Have your small salve containers ready and lined up with oils you want to use next to them. Also, have labels ready if you are a super organized person. Pour mixture into containers and it will start setting up within a minute or so, so make sure to drop Essential oils in at this time. Separate them according to which oil is used so you can add the correct oil used to each label.

► Use on skin anywhere on the body. It's healing properties help heal deep, cracked skin and heels.

My daughter and I love this salve for comfort, healing, and protection from elements.

Teeth: Clean and whiten teeth, and nourish gums with ***Protective Blend Toothpaste***. It contains ***Clove*** to help with sensitivity, ***Orange, Melaleuca*** (stops biofilms), ***Rosemary, Eucalyptus, Cinnamon Bark,*** Stevia for flavoring, hydrated silica for whitening, ***Myrrh*** for skin and gum health, ***Wintergreen*** for freshening.

You can also add baking soda on your toothbrush for alkalizing your mouth! It brings the Ph into balance, but only use once a week as it is abrasive and wears away enamel.

Hair: Use the ***Protective Shampoo*** and ***Smoothing Conditioner*** for stunning hair with essential oils!

Thoroughly brush the hair before shampooing to help strengthen the hair follicles and bring natural oils to the surface.

The shampoo is salon quality and very concentrated. You only need a pea-sized amount for shorter hair, and two pea-sized amounts for longer hair. Add plenty of water for a smooth, luxurious lather. Be sure to get all your hair up into the lather to remove dirt and toxins from open hair follicles. No need to shampoo again, as when you rinse the hair, it will be squeaky clean! (unless it's super, super dirty, then shampoo again, but normally not necessary)

After rinsing out shampoo, apply two teaspoons of smoothing conditioner and smooth it very thoroughly into all the hair with special attention to drier areas. Leave on for 2 minutes, then rinse out. Wrap head in towel, and allow heat to penetrate head, making the conditioner go deeper into hair follicles.

After damp-drying hair, apply serum on roots and tips of hair for more conditioning.

Use holding glaze, working into all the hair and style as usual or leave hair natural.

You will find your hair luxurious and pampered with extra shine and bounce. It will stay clean and bouncy for a few days!

CHAPTER 8
How to Detoxify Heavy Metals Safely & Easily with Cilantro & Zeolite

If you have never considered what you are about to read, don't feel like the Lone Ranger, (unless of course, you were a Ranger.) ha ha. When we first learned about the need for getting rid of heavy metals because of the negative effect on the body (particularly thyroid function), we were somewhat shocked. We learned how metals can plug receptor sites in the body, disrupting normal functions and wreaking havoc. AND we learned the easiest and simplest way to unload them.

There are two ways to do this directly; ***Cilantro oil***, and ***Zeolites***.

Check out this article on using only ***Cilantro*** (i.e. Cilantro oil) from www.drdavidwilliams.com :

"One of the best methods I've found for removing these toxins is what I call the "poor man's chelation therapy." Dr. Yoshiaki Omura with the Heart Research Foundation in New York discovered a unique and easy way to remove heavy metals like mercury, lead, and aluminum. He and his colleagues were using antibiotics and antiviral compounds to treat infections, but they were having little long-term success. Patients' symptoms would disappear, only to recur within a few months.

Upon further investigation Dr. Omura found that these patients had localized deposits of mercury, lead, aluminum, or a combination, and the infectious bacterial and viral agents continued to grow and multiply in these areas. Apparently, in the presence of these heavy metals, the antibiotics and antiviral compounds lost their ability to function.

While Dr. Omura was testing the urine of one patient, he discovered that mercury levels in the urine decreased significantly after the patient consumed Vietnamese soup, which contains cilantro.

Through further testing, Dr. Omura found that consumption of cilantro accelerated the excretion of lead and aluminum deposits from the body. When he had his patients regularly consume fresh cilantro or cilantro juice and then use antibiotics or natural antivirals such as the EPA and DHA in fish oil, the infections were permanently cleared.

Dr. Omura performed another study in which three amalgam fillings were removed from an individual using all the precautions available to prevent the absorption of mercury from the amalgam. Even with strong air and water suctioning, water rinses, and a rubber dental dam, significant amounts of mercury were later found in the individual's lungs, kidneys, endocrine organs, liver, and heart. There had been no mercury in these tissues prior to the amalgam removal. Using only cilantro, Dr. Omura was able to clear the mercury deposits in just three weeks. -"

♥ I have literally heard dozens of stories about how someone's urine had a metallic smell after using ***Cilantro*** oil.♥

►Use 4 drops per day in veggie cap.

►Use sparingly on dips and other foods

Companion oils: ***Coriander, Thyme, Cleansing Blend, Cypress, Cinnamon***

Be sure to take plenty of fiber & water while on any detox schedule to help bind toxins and die-off.

ZEOLITE

Negatively charged neurotoxins abound here at home with pollution. Without going into the gory details that could freak you out, suffice it to say, you need detoxification from pollution. Everyone does, not just warriors, but especially warriors! You guys have had vaccines, and been exposed to all kinds of junk.

It's very simple to take; an intra-oral spray. There are also versions of it online to buy, but you have to be cautious; not everything offered online is actual zeolite. We simply cannot keep this a secret from soldiers knowing its potential for removing toxins.

Zeolites are the 'best kept secret' for removing heavy metals. They are unique groupings of minerals with a 4-sided honeycomb structure and a ***negative magnetic charge***. This distinctive structure allows zeolite to capture ***positively charged*** heavy metals (i.e. aluminum, lead, mercury, etc), environmental toxins and free radicals. Zeolite has small cavities that contain these negatively charged compounds that strongly attract and capture toxins and free radicals.

Once zeolite captures toxins it then holds them with its magnetic energy until they are excreted out of the body through normal digestion. Approximately 60% of the excretion leaves through the urine and 40% through fecal matter.(see references for zeolite supplies)

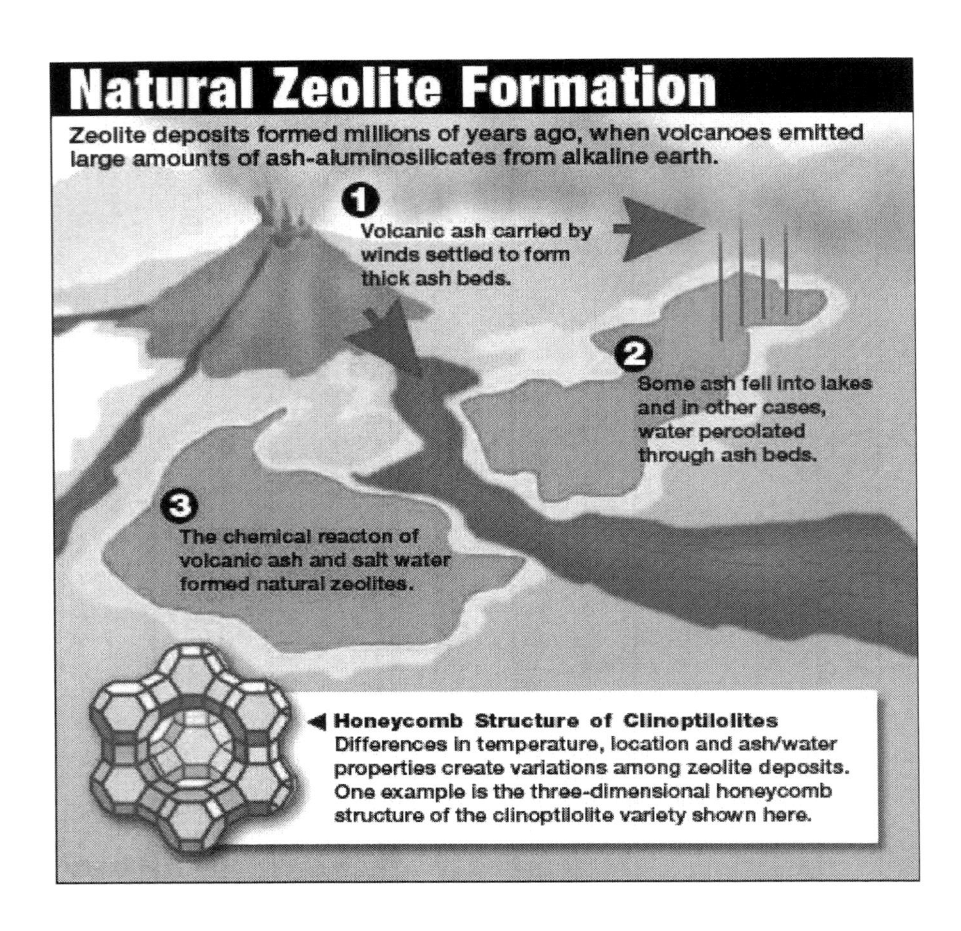

Graphic from JRDockers.com

CHAPTER 9
How to Address Post-War Stuff

◄MATTER has MEMORY ►

Matter has memory. What is meant by this? The best examples are computer devices and technology we use in everyday life that have data stored on them, which we easily access to serve us. The human body is much the same way as a device, but accessing emotional information is sometimes uncomfortable and difficult. For horrific memories that are stored, we would rather they go straight to the "Recycle Bin" so to speak. PTSD is not fun to live with or sort through.

BUT, hope is here! The opportunity to ease those memories in a different context is here. A tool for gentle and gradual re-processing of emotions is here. Essential oils provide a cushion for emotional memory events.

Every time you inhale an oil during a memory event, you *shift the impact* of that stored memory a little bit. In fact, even if you are not having a memory event, the consistent use of oils has a significant impact on emotional health. Inhaling oils, repetitively during the day, will ***gently, gradually*** begin to re-write the perception of that memory, via the limbic system. The limbic system is the place where emotional memories are stored and communicated through the body using SMELL. The memory is then stored in the brain, and at locations around the body. Hence, when I performed a massage table technique on my daughter as mentioned in Chapter 3, she released some stored memories in tissues along the spine. (The place where her spine was fractured from the explosion). This is one way to release emotions.

When emotion is released from the body, it's called catharsis. ***Catharsis is the process of releasing, and thereby providing relief from, strong or repressed emotions.*** Catharsis can be startling, at first coming out as tears or laughter, followed by a huge sense of relief. There is significant energy release with catharsis, then strong relaxation, or yawning. Some of the dread leaves us. We feel cleansed and washed on the inside. We feel more at peace with ourselves.

For Warriors, a lot of numbing out has taken place. Maybe you live in a constant state of denial: "don't talk, don't trust, don't feel." The idea that you can kill or be killed, has to be addressed to survive in a war. You've been conditioned to think and feel this way. You either become overwhelmed with grief and fear, or you understand you have to suppress all normal empathy and humanity to do your job. This is challenging to unpack once you're home because it is so deeply buried. You can't undo it easily. It is deeply personal. It becomes unbearable at times. Some of you have permanently ended the pain for yourselves forever.

We speak to the living: you need something that can be covert inside your very cells. You need help to align your humanity again. Essential oils will help. They are very tiny molecules that go in and are readily accepted by our bodies, because they are recognized as food—**SOUL FOOD** and **PHYSICAL FOOD** (10,000,000,000,000,000,000 molecules in one drop!). Your body knows they are natural and knows how to use them. They don't have to explain themselves to the body or disguise themselves....they are allowed to work. They are allies. They are 'troop support'. They are excellent for use with therapies. (speak with your doctor ☺)

The following is an alphabetical 'generic' list of common events associated with after-effects of living in a war zone and the oils to try. Use these suggestions as starting points of experiencing the oils. Everyone's body make-up is a little different, so adjustment may be needed here and there. A complete description of :

1. Oil Chemistry
2. Physical benefits
3. Emotional benefits

can be found in Modern Essentials book, 6th Edition, or online or see an abridged version in the APPENDIX.

PTSD NATURAL SOLUTIONS

Anger/Confusion

►Immediately put 2 drops ***Peppermint***, 2 drops ***Frankincense***, or any of the Soul Support Collection oils, on hands and cup over nose. Leave area and slow down. Do deep breathing ten times. Keep inhaling oils. Let anger pass before acting. Try to identify whether you are fearful, judgemental, or habitually angry. Talk to your therapist.

Remember that when agitated, the brain becomes starved of oxygen as the nervous system readies for attack-mode or danger. When the brain is not oxygenated properly, good decisions become harder to make, thus resulting in a poor outcome.

►Inhale ***Encouraging Blend, Melissa,*** or ***Grounding Blend***.

►Diffuse ***Bergamot*** or ***Respiratory Blend,*** or inhale straight from the bottle.

►Try *Tapping*. *Tapping* is a method of calming. Start by tapping on top of your head very lightly but firmly with one hand, using your fingertips. Tap repetitively many times for 30 seconds, then move to forehead for 30 seconds. Repeat affirmations out loud to yourself: "I am enough." "Even though I'm angry or afraid, I will love myself." "Even though I see no way out, I'm going to love myself," etc. Now move down to your cheekbones, and using both hands if possible, tap your cheekbones for 30 seconds. Keep saying affirmations to yourself, using your own positive ones, even if you don't believe them yet.

Move tapping to breastbones. Tap 30 more seconds. Then tap on your side under arm on your rib cage with one hand for 30 seconds. By now you should be getting calm. Keep tapping. Now move the tapping to the outside of your fist. If possible, tap the outside of your fist for 30 seconds. After you do all of these spots, start over if needed. You may have to do this twice, but, maybe not. Everyone is different. This is also very effective for any discomfort.

►Seek a massage table technique. (See Chapter 3)

Booming Sounds

►Gently massage 1 drop ***Helichrysum*** around outside of each ear. If you don't have it, combine one drop ***Basil*** with one drop ***Frankincense.***

►Inhale ***Lavender*** or ***Calming Blend*** to slow heart & soothe emotions. One or two drops of ***Ylang Ylang*** massaged over heart chakra will slow the heart from racing.

►Keep inhaling ***Lavender*** (or ***Calming blend***) until marked improvement. It could take a few minutes. If cold sweats are present inhale some ***Peppermint.***

Electrical 'brain-shock' Sensations

This sensation is associated with TBI (Traumatic Brain Injury). TBI's are present in like 90% of Post-War Effected people, but not everyone has this sensation. my daughter uses ***Frankincense*** to ward this off. She uses 2 drops ***Frankincense*** in the morning under her tongue before breakfast as a precaution, 2 drops before lunch, and 2-4 drops in the afternoon/evening. These sensations went from occurring 3 times a day, down to one a month using this protocol. Sometimes the sensation will appear with acute stress, at which point she then has more ***Frankincense*** given by someone present (like myself, if I am there when it occurs) and comes right out of it.

These are no fun. On the rare occasions they do happen, they are not fun to go through, or standby and witness. We are so happy we have something to use that is fast, safe, and effective.

►Use 2-4 drops of ***Frankincense*** under the tongue up to 4 times per day, depending on feelings.

►Use 1-2 drops ***Peppermint*** to cool effects.

Fatigue

Fatigue, i.e. adrenal exhaustion, can be very insidious. It's gradual sapping of our energy leaves us feeling drained and not easily able to regain vitality from rest. Especially when it takes everything we've got just to function in the world emotionally. Physically low energy vibration because of a cold or flu, chronic illness, menstruation, depression, etc., can play significant roles in adrenal vitality, thus zapping us of our precious energy cushion. Of course, taking the ***Basic Vitality Supplements*** will help greatly (Chapter 1). Also, a massage table technique is in order for restoring homeostasis. (See Chapter 3 for details).

CAUTION: *More is better, right?? NOT. Use a little at a time, EASY DOES IT. Take as suggested.*

Basil~

►Use 2 drops in a 16 oz glass of water. Use a fork to stir and break up the oil drops in the water. Drink. You can also add 1 drop ***Peppermint*** or 1 drop ***Geranium*** for enhanced benefit.

►Put 3 drops into a veggie capsule and swallow with lots of water if you don't care for taste in glass of water.

►Rub a drop on bottom of each foot at bedtime.

►Diffuse in occupied home or work area.

Rosemary ~

►Use 2 drops in a 16 oz glass of water. Use a fork to stir and break up the oil drops in the water. Drink. You can also add 1 drop ***Peppermint*** for extra 'POW' effect.

►Massage 2 drops on bottom of each foot at bedtime for adrenal exhaustion or fatigue.

►Inhale straight from bottle, or put in diffuser for occupied room.

Thyme~

►Massage on tired parts of body, diluted 1:1. Combine with 1:1 ***Bergamot*** or 1:1 ***Meluleuca*** for added benefit. Remember, these oils are strong; always start with one drop! You can always add more. "Less, more often" is the motto ☺

►Can be added to bathwater. About 5 drops, agitate water to break up oil and disperse better.

Fear ~

Fear, terror, anxiousness can all play on each other. Most of the time we endure the "false" kind of fear; meaning we are not really in danger. Our perceptions may be skewed, but we act and make decisions as though we ARE in danger. Fear can be insidious and something that lies just under the surface all the time, constantly in the background of everything we do. This can be a hold-over from childhood, or a result of situations in adulthood, or both. First, we need to be able to identify it, so we can deal with it.

Recognizing emotions is crucial for growth (Appendix 4). Fear makes us have a shorter breathing pattern, which cuts off oxygen from the brain. Sometimes we only can decipher just maybe three of four emotions at first. (See emotion list in Appendix) Whatever our fear is caused by, we can start using oils to gradually help us overcome it at a cellular level.

►Diffuse ***Cassia, Cinnamon, Birch, Cypress, Lavender, Myrrh, Vetiver. Soul Support Collection.***

►***Cassia*** and ***Cinnamon*** MUST be diluted 1:1 with a carrier oil like fractionated coconut oil, or olive oil. Put 1 drop ***Cassia*** or ***Cinnamon*** on feet diluted. Massage in.

►Use one drop ***Cinnamon*** in a morning smoothie using your blender. Or make these yummy chips: **doterrablog.com/diy-cinnamon-apple-chips-with-doterra-essential-oils/**

►Refer to Chapter Two.

►***Cinnamon*** and ***Cassia*** are in the same family of oils and are considered "hot" to the skin. Be sure to dilute. (***Cassia*** is about ½ the price of ***Cinnamon***)

Birch ~

►Diffuse and inhale. Inspiring aroma. Clears airways and breathing while stimulating the mind and enhancing focus.

►Apply one drop to brain stem and massage in for fears.

►Use topically on sore muscles or ligaments.

Cypress ~

Cypress is very helpful in making things flow again: be it emotions or blood or toxins. Great for draining lymph glands during lymphatic drain therapy. Really helps with bone spurs and carpal tunnel.

►Use on scars and shrapnel sites, bone spur sites. Be consistent with it.

►Use to help life flow again! Use topically 1 drop on each foot sometime during the day.

►Use on temples, 1 drop, or along with 1 drop ***Frankincense*** for calming and release. Especially during onset of anxious events.

Lavender ~

This oil is part of the FLiP TRINITY of OILS: ***Frankincense, Lavender,*** and ***Peppermint.*** It has a major calming effect for any anxious situations. My daughter keeps some at her bedside, and in the glovebox for driving. She also bathes in it before bed. Can be sensually enhancing.

►Massage 1 drop around outer ear if awakened with nightmare.

►Diffuse in occupied rooms for anxiety

►Can be used in recipes like cakes and cookies. Can be applied NEAT (no dilution) but always use care as they are very concentrated molecules ☺

Myrrh ~

►Use 1-2 drops on skin for emotional support and skin issues.

►Inhale when feeling triggered or afraid.

►Great for foot fungus issues, skin issues, flaky skin, itchy skin. Ok for outer genitalia. Always try a little diluted first.

►Enjoy the exotic richness of this oil!

Vetiver ~

Vetiver can be a great choice for triggers. However, not everyone responds in the same way to it. Try ***Reassuring Blend*** for triggers, or your favorite oil. Sometimes all that is needed is to inhale an oil to "shift" the trigger.

►Massage 1 drop on back of hands to inhale during the day.

<u>Feet</u>

The feet are good places to absorb any oils, because the pores are large, and oils don't need to be AS diluted when used on the feet because of calluses.

►Use 2 drops ***Arborvitae*** on toe fungus. Or ***Clove, Meluleuca,*** or ***Oregano.***

►Use 2 drops ***Protective Blend*** in bottom of shower or bathtub after use for stopping threats.

►Use Stink-foot powder Recipe after bath.

Grief & Loss

Grief is a feeling of severe loss and depression due to that loss. In my case grief was closely tied to remorse and regret; remorse over making bad decisions, or losing relationships due to death or conflict, and then having a great deal of depressed grief. There are basically five transitions with grief. You kind of have to decide where you currently are to begin with, and everyone's time frame is different.

- *Denial and Isolation, or numbing out to the situation.* Example: I couldn't believe I had lost my brother, a Viet Nam Vet, and my fiancee, in a single motorcycle accident. I was in shock for 6 months.

- *Anger.* Feeling pain and directing, or I should say 'deflecting it' onto someone or something else. Example: I vowed never to ride a motorcycle again. Obviously, had they been in a car, they would probably have survived. The guy driving the car that slammed into them survived!
- *Bargaining.* This part is "If only I...." Example: If only I had not let Vance get on the motorcycle. If only I had been able to kiss him goodbye. If only we hadn't gone to his house that day.
- *Depression.* Sadness. Tears. Lamenting. I could not stop crying for several months. It was like riding a wave sometimes, that would hit me after I smelled his cologne, (I had saved some of Vance's shirts and would bury my face in them, just to remind myself of my love for him and cry more!)
- *Acceptance.* The thought that life is never going to be the same, and somehow I would survive. But here I bargained some more, promising I would never find another love like Vance. For the loss of my brother, I would never ride another motorcycle again. I have never stopped missing them.

Grief and loss do not mean anything is wrong with us. In fact, in our humble opinion, it means we are feeling natural and being human. It's part of our humanity to feel grief and loss at times. There are "pearls" of healing inside of grief and loss, if we allow it. With the loss of my Dad, a lot of emotion was tied to the thought of him. I couldn't even speak his name without tears coming, until the "pearl" came one day. For three years after his loss, I had a nagging feeling in the back of my mind that he had somehow possibly been buried alive. I was imagining him clawing the inside of his coffin, and calling for help. After grief work I realized that it was our 'unfinished emotional business' that was actually clawing to get out and be resolved! My mind put it together for me when I allowed the feelings to speak to me instead of stuffing them. I had received my 'pearl'. Now I am totally emotionally free from all troubling feelings of him.

►Diffuse ***Comforting Blend***, or any ***Soul Support Collection*** oil, in occupied areas 24/7. Alternate them, but keep them going for intense grief memories. You have to sort this out for yourself, but trust your intuition on how you feel. Keep oils with you and on you while you are working through the intensity of it.

►Alternate diffusing ***Lemon, Joyful Blend, Invigorating Blend*** in occupied areas.

►Apply 2 drops ***Grounding Blend*** to bottoms of feet in the morning. Put a note on your fridge to remind yourself to use the oils.

►Apply ***Ylang-Ylang*** over heart chakra.

►For courage to do the work: 1 drop ***Helichrysum*** over heart, inhalation of ***Birch***, and/or use 3 drops ***Cassia*** in a veggie cap, swallow with lots of water.

►Diffuse ***Invigorating Blend*** and ***Joyful Blend*** in occupied areas, wear on oils pendant.

Survivor's Guilt

Guilt plays a HUGE part of grief, if our decisions helped cause the loss, or we made it through when others didn't. It's difficult to make it to the acceptance phase. DO NOT GIVE UP HOPE OF FINDING A NEW WAY OF BEING with your situation. It will happen.

Photo courtesy of realwarriors.net

►Reach out to another Warrior to talk to.

► Diffuse ***Joyful Blend*** in occupied areas or inhale straight from bottle.

► Apply ***Deep Soothing Blend*** to outer earlobes.

► Massage 2 drops ***Orange*** on bottoms of feet at bedtime. Wear oils pendant with ***Orange*** on it. Mix with a drop of ***Frankincense***. Diffuse ***Orange*** in areas too.

► Diffuse ***Renewing Blend***, or your favorite ***Soul Support Collection*** oil.

Hot Brain

Confusion, agitation, and fight or flight mechanisms are typical occurrences before or after "events". ***Peppermint*** has a unique cooling property which makes it a good choice for hotness.

► Use 1-2 drops ***Peppermint*** on upper forehead for cooling. Also on back of neck.

► Put 2 drops in 20 oz glass of water with ice, and drink!

► Put 1 drop ***Frankincense,*** 1 drop ***Lavender*** and massage over heart. Cup hands over nose and inhale.

► Take 1 drop ***Melissa*** under tongue.

Hypervigilance

This feeling is accompanied by nervousness, perhaps paranoia, claustrophobic feelings, memory events. Use the Emotions List if needed to separate feelings.

Experiment and rotate use with the eleven oils below. Start with one or two that smell good, and work your way through them. Remember, "Less, More Often" is the rule of thumb. Consistent use is much better.

► Roll ***Focus Blend*** on wrists and rub together. Roll it on brain stem.

► Put 1 drop ***Frankincense*** and 1 drop ***Melissa*** under tongue.

► Put 1 drop ***Patchouli*** on each temple and inhale.

► Massage the ***Massage Blend*** on outer earlobes.

► Apply one drop ***Marjoram*** on tight muscle groupings.

► Diffuse ***Cilantro*** or ***Protective Blend*** alternately by the hour in occupied areas.

► Apply one drop ***Peppermint*** to forehead and or neck periodically as tolerated.

► Apply ***Ylang-Ylang***, 1 drop over heart chakra.

► Use 5 drops ***Roman Chamomile***, and 1 cup Epsom Salts in warm, soothing bath.

Photo courtesy realwarriors.net

"There's an Oil for that."

Isolation (accompanied by Avoidance)

Sometimes accompanied by avoidance, this is very common with PTSD. Some of it is shame to be around others for fear of embarrassing them, or the fear of being with people because of mistrust, or anything. This feeling also curtails daily responsibilities such as picking up the mail, opening mail, making/returning phone calls, answering the door, paying bills, cooking, socializing. Don't take this personally if you are a close family member. It takes tremendous thought and forthright decision-making to move out of isolation and find people to relate to. Another Warrior is a good start.

The following are some suggested oils that help energetically and emotionally. All the oils have a distinct vibrational frequency, thus they are homeopathic solutions in their own rite.

►Diffuse ***Reassuring Blend*** or ***Renewing Blend*** in occupied areas.

►Massage 1-2 drops ***Cypress*** on calves and feet. Inhale from bottle.

►Apply ***Patchouli*** to temples and inhale or 1 drop in navel.

►Use ***Deep Soothing Blend*** on achy muscles and joints for comforting self.

►Massage 1 drop ***Helichrysum*** over heart chakra.

►Apply 2 drops ***Grounding Blend*** on bottoms of feet upon rising.

►Diffuse ***Marjoram, Lemon***, or ***Invigorating Blend*** in occupied areas.

►Apply 2 drops ***Black Peppermint Blend**** over stomach for comforting upset digestive tract.

►Diffuse ***Reassuring Blend***.

►Consider writing down affirmations from APPENDIX and pasting them around home. It's surprising how much it helps.

Loss of Smell

►Inhale ***Eucalyptus***, or ***Respiratory Blend*** from bottle. Do this daily.

►Inhale ***Basil*** from bottle. Do this often. Also dilute 1:1 and apply on nose tip.

Mental Chatter

To curb mental chatter or the voices that just won't 'shut up' in our heads:

►Apply 2 drops ***Vetiver*** to brain stem. Apply one drop to bottom of each foot, and into navel.

►Roll on ***Focus Blend*** over forehead. Repeat every 15 minutes if needed.

Metal & Sulfur Smells

These odors can trigger an event.

►Immediately use ½ drop ***Eucalyptus*** under nose. Or ***Respiratory Blend***. Just swipe top of bottle with finger and apply under nose to shift brain. Continue using, applying a drop to backs of hands, and on chest.

Nausea

►Use ***Ginger*** diluted 1:1 on tummy area. It's strong and warming. If it gets too warm, dilute with more FCO.

►Use 1 drop ***Fennel*** under tongue. Has a minty, licorice taste that's very sweet.

►Use 1 drop ***Digestive Blend*** under tongue, or directly on tummy. Dilute for sensitive persons. Use more drops if needed.

Out-of-Body Feeling (euphoria)

No one is certain what brings this on, but it does exist. It can cause panic if it is associated in the brain with feeling no pain, hence leaving one to question 'am I still alive, or have I left my body and reality'? Fortunately, it doesn't last long, maybe a minute or so.

►After warning the person, use a drop or two of ***Black Pepper.***

►Use ***Black Peppermint*** combo topically along spine.

►Apply 2 drops ***Grounding Blend*** to bottom of each foot, and inhale from bottle.

Ringing in the Ears

►Massage either 1 drop ***Helichrysum*** around outer ear every 30 minutes until noticeable difference occurs. OR

►Combine 1 drop ***Basil*** and 1 drop ***Frankincense***, and massage around outer ears.

►Use box fan on low setting when sleeping, if tolerable, to drown sounds. It's called 'White Noise".

Sleeplessness

All efforts should be made to create a "before sleep" routine....even if it sort of 'fails' at first.

►Begin by inhaling ***Calming Blend*** or ***Lavender*** when you first think of sleep (an hour before attempting sleep).

►If possible, draw a bath, using 5 drops ***Lavender***, 3 drops ***Helichrysum***, ½ cup Epsom Salts, and ½ cup Baking Soda. Soak in bath for at least 20 minutes.

►At bedtime, massage 2 drops ***Lavender*** or ***Calming Blend*** on bottoms of feet. Cover them with cotton socks. Take 2 ***DNA Repair Blend*** soft gels, or apply 2 drops of the oil version on bottoms of feet.

►Keep PTSD Trinity oils at bedside for use if awakened at night.

►Absolutely ESSENTIAL, is keeping the diffuser going at bedside with your favorite relaxing oil. Try *tapping* as explained in ANGER/CONFUSION section.

Shrapnel

This is such a bugger! You cannot have an M.R.I. to pinpoint where it is because the magnets in the machine would tear the shrapnel straight out of the body, possibly ripping through vital organs!

We have struggled with this for my daughter, but since using oils and some techniques for removal, it's better! Back during Civil War days, physicians used ***Oregano*** oil on the battlefield for antiseptic. So, we started using ***Oregano*** for shrapnel. She took a capsule a day internally, plus diluted and rubbed it topically on shrapnel sites. The shrapnel came to the surface easier and quicker.

She had/has scarring at some sites that has a tendency to tighten and pull. In that case, because the VA hospital is so far away, and difficult to get into, I have had to sterilize a new razor blade, and gently slice the adhesions to release them. It works great. It's already numb, but you can use ***Clove*** mixed with ***Oregano*** at site to keep it numb and germ-free. (We have had to do this on many occasions, too.) My daughter is so damn tough!

►Mix 1 drop ***Oregano***, 1 drop ***Clove*** with 3 drops FCO, and apply to sites. Also, take 3 drops ***Oregano***, 2 drops ***Cilantro***, 3 drops FCO in a veggie cap and swallow with LOTS of water. If capsule breaks open in esophagus, it can kind of burn because of ***Oregano***. If it does, take an FCO chaser!

►Gently rinse area with saline after emergence. Use a SMALL magnet to attract emerging pepper spray shrapnel. Gently wipe with damp, clean towel. Bandage area. Talk with your physician.

Suicidal thoughts

This is a subject not to be messed around with. If someone is thinking or talking about suicide, please take this very serious. Professional help is critical. See your therapist or physician.

►Diffuse ***Frankincense*** in occupied areas, and put several drops under tongue.

►Consider getting a PTSD service dog:

http://www.pawsforveterans.com/

►Apply all three Trinity oils topically on bottoms of feet immediately at emergency.

►Call 1 (800) 273-8255, press 1; available 24 hours a day/7 days a week **http://www.veteranscrisisline.net/**

►Take the self-check quiz: **https://www.vetselfcheck.org/Welcome.cfm**

Teeth clenching

Grinding at night or clenching during the day because of stress is damaging to teeth and causes headaches. See if you can acquire a bite-guard.

►Use ***Calming Blend*** along jawline topically at bedtime. Diffuse it also at bedside.

►Put ***Deep Soothing Blend*** drops on jaws during daytime.

►Practice steady breathing in and out until shoulders and tension begin to relax.

Triggers

These are caused by the brain remembering something through the five senses: sight, smell, touch, taste, hearing. The #1 oil for this is ***Vetiver***.

Vetiver has a real 'grounding' effect, maybe because it is distilled from a ROOT system. It has an 'earthy-smell' to it, kind of like you are walking through a huge forest, taking in the earth beneath your feet. At first you may not care for its odor, but please have it on hand at all times.

►Put a drop of ***Vetiver*** on backs of hands. Inhale from bottle, or diffuse.

►Cup hands over nose and inhale. This will 'bring you back' right away.

►Inhale or diffuse ***Comforting Blend***. Apply 2 drops over the heart.

You may want to experiment on which oil is right for you when triggered. The sooner the better in using your oils at this time.

CHAPTER 10
Reintegration at Home

Reintegration takes time, too. Friends, family, and loved ones will try really hard to make you feel loved and at home at first. But then later, may not be able to be supportive enough, or TOO supportive.

From realwarriors.net:

- *Warriors returning home from deployment may experience challenges when reintegrating into civilian life due to survival skills they have developed while living in a combat environment. Below are eight battlefield skills that families can educate themselves about to better understand the common reintegration challenges of returning service members.*
- ***Safety.*** *Military personnel in the war zone must be on constant alert for danger. Everyday events at home, like a traffic jam, can trigger a sense of danger and vulnerability. The service member may seek constant control and vigilance or attempt to avoid these situations altogether. Those accustomed to living in a safe and secure environment may find these attitudes and behaviors difficult to understand.*
- ***Trust and Identifying the Enemy.*** *To survive, military personnel must learn quickly not to automatically trust in the war zone. It's better to assume that everyone is the enemy until proven otherwise. At home, mistrust and suspiciousness can severely damage the most important relationships, including marriage.*

- ***Mission Orientation.*** *The primary task in the military is to complete the mission ordered from above. All attention and resources are directed to its completion. In the civilian world, individuals are expected to take initiative, seek out tasks, balance competing priorities and decide for themselves how to proceed.*
- ***Decision Making.*** *In the war zone, following orders is critical to personal safety, the well-being of comrades and the success of the mission. Military personnel whose rank requires decision making must give life-and-death orders, even when all the information is not available. At home, especially in families, decision making tends to be cooperative. People take time to consider questions and options and to seek out additional information.*
- ***Response Tactics.*** *In the war zone, survival depends on automatic response to danger. It is critical to act first — with maximum firepower — and think later. Keeping all supplies and equipment, including weapons, clean, well-maintained and in their proper place is critical to response. At home, messy rooms and dirty dishes can feel dangerous, and the service member's response to these realities may appear as an over-reaction and can intimidate or even frighten family members.*
- ***Predictability and Intelligence Control.*** *In the war zone, troops are in serious danger if the enemy can predict their movements, routine, location or intentions. Military personnel learn to vary their routine and withhold information. But at home in a civilian environment, employers expect routines and children need them.*
- ***Emotional Control.*** *Combat exposes military personnel to overwhelming events that elicit fear, loss and grief. Yet the job requires that they move on quickly, staying alert and vigilant. The range of acceptable emotions may narrow to anger and numbness. Drugs and alcohol help sustain*

emotional numbing, even after the service member comes home. Emotions that are dangerous in combat are critical for relationships at home. (In my opinion, and experience, this emotional numbing can be a held over survival trait from living in an emotionally numbed and dysfunctional family—ours was dysfunctional for sure—and we pass it on unintentionally to our kids. We try hard not to, but it happens. Then after joining the military, they do well, because they only had a few identifiable emotions from the start! This is one reason we put the Emotions List in Appendix so this work of sorting out emotions can begin.)

- ***Talking about the War.*** *It's hard to talk about how the war changed the individual. War may challenge the service member's core beliefs about humanity and justice in the world. There are few opportunities to reflect on this in the combat situation. At home, it is difficult to explain to civilians — to people who live in safety — what happened in combat, what decisions were made, why those decisions were necessary. Talking about the war may overwhelm the service member with horror or grief. And service members may be afraid that their stories will upset people they care about or lead to rejection. To access additional information about reintegration challenges, resources and solutions for returning warriors in your family, use the resources below:*
- *Contact a trained health resource consultant at the DCoE Outreach Center by using Real Warriors Live Chat or by calling 866-966-1020.*
- *Read **"Returning from the War Zone: A Guide for Families of Military Members,"** [PDF 964KB] published by VA's National Center for PTSD.*

►Keep using FLiP Trinity oils.

►Diffuse ***Frankincense, Lavender, Orange,*** in occupied areas.

►Inhale ***Rosemary*** from bottle or diffuse.

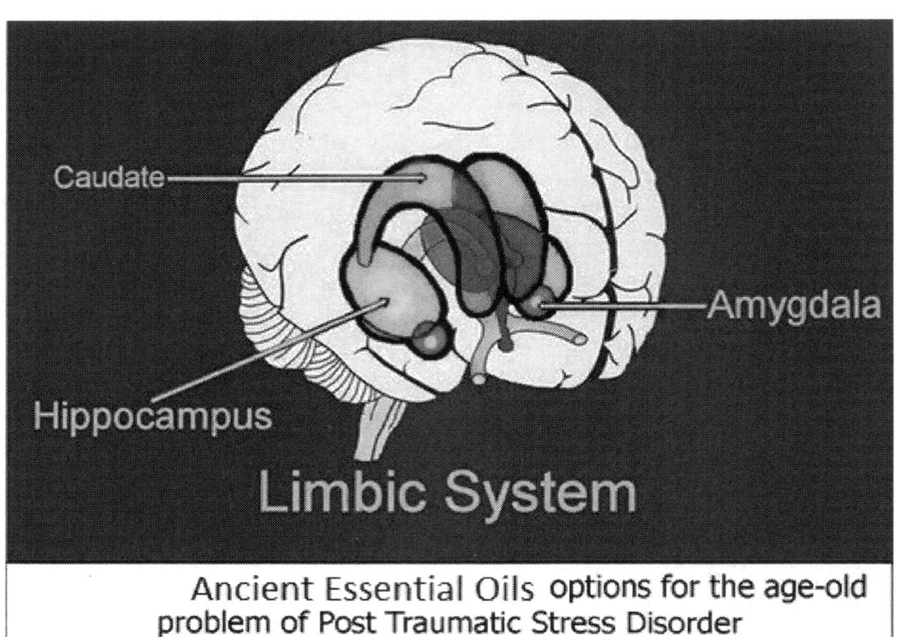

Ancient Essential Oils options for the age-old problem of Post Traumatic Stress Disorder

CHAPTER 11
Finding Your New Normal

The idea here is, there is no 'getting back to normal' per se. It's not about picking up where we left off exactly, but more like, how can I CREATE a new life with my new awareness and experiences of the rest of the real world. Sometimes, this becomes "low-crawl," feeling your way for years, avoiding dealing with adjustment.

It's going to take a while to learn how to "be" in civilian life now. That is understandable. The inertia of everything seems to hit AFTER returning home. Please, contact a 'Battle Bud' you can be yourself with, and talk to.

► Use oils for emotional support, especially the versatility of the FLiP Trinity of oils, ***Lavender, Frankincense and Peppermint.*** A lot of men, particularly, who were resistant to trying oils, are now our biggest users!

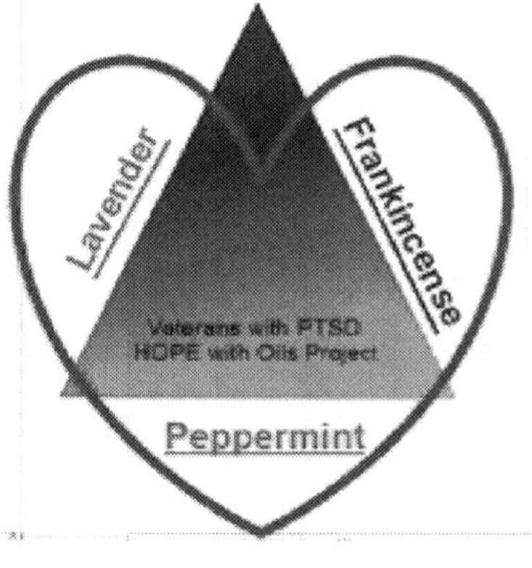

► Inhale ***Rosemary*** or diffuse in occupied areas for assistance in transitions.

► Take ***Detoxification Blend*** in a veggie cap, 3 drops every other day.

► Massage 1 drop ***Cellular Complex*** on each foot at bedtime, or take soft gels as indicated on bottle.

But please, don't put off getting therapy because the oils are helping you cope; this would be a huge mistake. Your mission now is to reintegrate the best you can for TODAY. Keep in close touch with your physicians and therapists. Oils support this in every way but are not a substitute for good therapy.

PTSD causes hesitation in reaching out of our comfort zones. But we must reach out, and make a decision to connect with others. Video games and social media are not a replacement for human contact. Calling a friend is a great start. I hope you will get comfort and encouragement from the oils, using them as a medium that will enable you to re-bond with family members.

Some more tools:

YOGA: yoga has many medical benefits like improved circulation and sleep. It can give you back a sense of 'being in control' of yourself again. Here is a site dedicated to Vets with YouTube video:

http://thereandbackagain.org

YOU ARE GOING TO MAKE IT. Do not give up. Refuse to Sink! You are going to be a new version of yourself!!

EMDR: **http://www.emdria.org/?gclid=CIil4Y6cusUDFW4Q7AodGjMAMg**

SELF-ADMINISTERED EMDR:

https://www.youtube.com/watch?v=OIfQIRJEsYk

ZYTO: **http://zyto.com/**

APPENDIX 1
Essential Oil Descriptions:

ANTI-AGING BLEND

Various distillations from bark, stems, resins

• Promotes healthy looking skin • Has calming and balancing properties • Promotes skin clarity, reduces appearance of spots and discoloration Excellent for scarring because this blend naturally promotes skin clarity!

A pre-blended oil of ***Patchouli, Bergamot, Sandalwood, Rose, Jasmine, Cinnamon Bark, Cistus, Vetiver, Ylang-Ylang, Geranium, Cocoa Bean Extract, and Vanilla Bean extract)***

We use this for perfume!! Comes in a 5ml bottle, and makes you feel Divine.

►Use 1-4 drops around neck, chest, inner thighs, navel.

ARBORVITAE

Steam distillation from heartwood

• Protects against environmental and seasonal threats • Promotes healthy cell function • Powerful cleansing and purifying agent • Natural insect repellent • Protects the body from harmful elements while supporting normal cell activity • Protects against common threats in the environment • Used by Native Americans for health benefits

We use it for toe fungus. It has a very woody, cedar-like smell to it. Native Americans use it for spiritual enhancement, and physical ailments.

Additional Research from the Modern Essentials Book, 6th ED.:
Anti-cancer properties: Hinokitiol was found to induce autophagic signaling in murine breast and colorectal tumor cells in vitro (Wang et al., 2014). Mice implanted with human colon cancer tumor cells saw a decrease in tumor size and weight when treated with ß-thujaplicin (hinokitiol) (Lee et al., 2013)

BASIL

Steam distilled from leaves, stems, flowers.

• Soothes sore muscles and joints • Assists with clear breathing • Acts as a cooling agent for the skin • Promotes mental alertness • Lessens anxious feelings • Enhances memory function • Reduces stress and tension • Reduces tension when applied to temples and back of neck • Soothes minor irritations • Sharpens focus while studying or reading • Soothes minor skin irritations

Basil has a herbaceous, spicy scent. ***Basil*** is what to use for general fatigue; a feeling of tiredness, due to over work or emotional stress.

Feeling weak or tired is an unmistakable feeling. Nagging tiredness could be a sign of adrenal wear and tear. Very good for those who are emotionally drained.

►Use 2 drops in a 16 oz glass of water. Use a fork to stir and break up the oil drops around the water. Drink. You can also add 1 drop ***Peppermint*** for extra 'POW' effect.

►Put 3 drops into a veggie capsule and swallow with lots of water if you don't care for taste in glass of water.

►Rub a drop on bottom of each foot at bedtime.

►Diffuse in occupied home or work area.

Additional Research from Modern Essentials Book, 6th Ed.:

Basil oil was found to strongly inhibit several multi-drug resistant bacteria (Opalchenova et al., 2003)

Basil extract was found to inhibit the growth of MCF-7 breast cancer cells, possess antioxidant activity, and protect against DNA damage (Al-Ai et al., 2013

BERGAMOT

Pressed from rind or peel; rectified and void of terpenes

• Calming and soothing aroma • Frequently used in massage therapy for its calming benefits

Kind of looks like a lime crossed with a lemon, but has a uniquely different aroma.

► Diffuse in the classroom, at work, or at home when stress levels or tension is high.

► Apply to the skin while showering and inhale deeply to experience its calming aroma while enjoying its purifying skin benefits.

► Change regular tea to Earl Grey with the addition of ***Bergamot***.

► Apply to the feet before bedtime for a sense of calm and harmony.

► Add 1-2 drops to your next DIY skin care cleanser.

► Mixes well with ***Lavender, Patchouli, Lime,*** and ***Arborvitae.***

► Diffuse for a sense of self-confidence.

BIRCH

Steam distillation from wood.

Similar to ***Wintergreen, Birch*** has a sweet, spicy, and minty aroma, rich in methyl salicylate (topical pain relief analgesic) • Frequently used in massage therapy and to soothe sore muscles and joints • Supports healthy circulation • Promotes clear breathing and healthy respiratory function • Beneficial for oily skin conditions

• Stimulating aroma promotes feelings of strength, warmth, and vitality

Birch is very effective in promoting circulation, making it ideal for massage therapy and to soothe sore joints and muscles.

►Diffuse and inhale. Inspiring aroma. Clears airways and breathing while stimulating the mind and enhancing focus.

►Apply 1 drop to brain stem and massage in for fears.

►Use topically on sore muscles or ligaments.

BLACK PEPPER~'Poor Man's Melissa Oil'

Steam distilled from berries.

Rich source of antioxidants • Supports healthy circulation *Aids digestion *Comforting and stimulating *For environmental and seasonal threats

Additional Research from Modern Essentials Book, 6th Ed.:

Inhaled vapor of black pepper oil was found to reduce cravings for cigarettes and symptoms of anxiety in smokers deprived of smoking compared to a control (Rose et al., 1994)

Inhalation of black pepper oil was found to increase cerebral blood flow and to improve the swallowing reflex in elderly patients who had suffered a stroke (Ebihara et al., 2006)

BLEND FOR WOMEN

Various distillations

• Combines with each individual's chemistry to create a beautiful, unique, and personal fragrance • Provides a warming, musky aroma that entices the senses and intrigues the mind • Calms the skin and emotions

A pre-blended oil of ***Patchouli, Bergamot, Sandalwood, Rose, Jasmine, Cinnamon Bark, Cistus, Vetiver,***

Ylang-Ylang, Geranium, Cocoa Bean Extract, and Vanilla Bean extract)

We use this for perfume!! Comes in a 5ml bottle, and makes you feel Divine.

►Use 1-4 drops around neck, chest, inner thighs, navel.

►Use 4 drops in bath for calming, sensuality.

CASSIA

A close relative to ***Cinnamon***, ***Cassia*** has a strong, spicy aroma that can be used in small quantities to transform any essential oil blend. ***Cassia*** has been used for thousands of years to maintain physical health and promote emotional well-being. It's one of the few essential oils mentioned in the Old Testament, noted for its unmistakable fragrance and calming properties. ***Cassia*** is a "warming" oil that helps promote circulation while maintaining healthy immune function. It can also aid in digestion, lessen nausea, and is a great oil to diffuse during cold months due to its warming properties and spicy scent. ****Due to its caustic nature, ***Cassia*** should be diluted with Fractionated Coconut Oil when applied to the skin and can be very strong when inhaled directly.****

When diluted, ***Cassia*** can help soothe sore, achy joints.

Cassia can be used in cooking either as a replacement for ***Cinnamon*** in pies and breads or by itself in a myriad of entrees and desserts.

► Add one drop to citrus blends. (not a great one for diffusing all by itself, because its so strong)

► Take one to two drops in veggie capsules for added immune support when seasonal threats are high.

► Combine one drop with ***Fractionated Coconut Oil*** and apply to sore, achy joints.

► Put 1 drop on TBSP (tablespoon) honey. Combine with 1 drop ***Lemon*** in 8oz warm water for comforting drink.

Additional Research from Modern Essentials Book, 6th Ed:

Anxiety: A single treatment of Cassia extract decreased anxiety in mice by causing a change of serotonin receptors in the dorsal raphe nucleous (Jung et al., 2012)

Male Impotence: Methanol extract of cassia was found to effectively manage sexual dysfunction in aged rats. (Goswami et al., 2014)

CALMING BLEND

Various methods of distillation

• Calming, renewing fragrance • Promotes relaxation and restful sleep • Diffuses into a subtle aroma, ideal for aromatic benefits • Lessens tension and calms emotions • Helps reduce worry and stress

This blend of oil is perfect for anxious teeth grinding, calming, mood swings, tension, stress.

Contains Lavender, Sweet Marjoram, Roman Chamomile, Ylang Ylang, Sandalwood, Vanilla Bean Extract. Skin test yourself first if using topically, on inside of elbow. Try ½ drop there first and wait a few minutes to see if it's irritating.

For those who don't care for the strong scent of straight ***Lavender*** by itself, this is the blend to try. It has a mellower aroma to it. Many people suffering from Post-War stuff, love this oil for promoting sleep and calm feelings. Blends provide a great way to try oils when you are first starting out because you are not buying them each individually. But as you become more in-tune with the oils and more skilled at your body, you will want to buy them individually too.

►Inhale straight from bottle during onset of stress. Diffuse in occupied areas.

►Massage 2 drops on bottom of each foot at bedtime and cover with cotton sock. Also, you may want to diffuse at bedtime. Try one or the other first, and do more if needed. Can also be applied straight on filter of CPAP machine.

►Can be worn as perfume or cologne. Mix with White Fir for masculine scent. See R.I.P blend recipe.

CELLULAR COMPLEX

A strong blend of ***Frankincense, Orange, Lemongrass, Thyme, Summer Savory, Clove, Niaouli.***

• Supports healthy cellular integrity by helping to reduce oxidative stress • Supports healthy cellular function and metabolism • Protects the body and cells from oxidative stress

This blend is good at supporting cellular "die off" meaning that it helps the body expel dead cells. Which is good! My daughter uses it at bedtime to support good sleep.

See Aromaticscience.com for studies on each individual oil in this blend!

CILANTRO

Steam distillation from leaves

(same plant as Coriander oil, which is distilled from seeds)

• Rich in antioxidants • Aids digestion • Powerful cleanser and **detoxifier** • Soothing to the skin • Gives food a fresh and tasty flavor

This is your #1 oil for cleansing. It has a herbaceous, citrusy, fresh scent. Some people really don't like it, so for them it can be taken internally in a veggie capsule.

►Use 4 drops per day in veggie cap.

►Use sparingly on dips and other foods

► **Be sure to take plenty of fiber while on any detox schedule to help bind and eliminate toxins and die-off.**

Companion oils: Coriander, Thyme, Cleansing Blend, Cypress, Cinnamon

These statements have not been evaluated by the Food and Drug Administration. This product is not intended to diagnose, treat, cure, or prevent any disease.

CINNAMON BARK

Cinnamon is derived from a tropical, evergreen tree that grows up to 45 feet high and has highly fragrant bark, leaves, and flowers. Extracted from bark, cinnamon oil contains strong cleansing and immune enhancing properties. Due to its high content of cinnamaldehyde, ***Cinnamon*** should be diluted with ***Fractionated Coconut Oil*** when applied to the skin and only one to two drops are needed for internal benefits.

♥ ***Cinnamon*** is very purifying to the circulatory system, helping promote circulation, both internally and when applied to the skin, and helping to ease sore muscles and joints.♥ ***Cinnamon*** helps maintain a healthy immune system, especially when seasonal threats are high. When diffused, Cinnamon promotes clear breathing while purifying the air.

► Antibacterial, anti-depressant

► Use as you would ***Cassia***

► Sensual enhancer

Additional Research from Modern Essentials Book, 6th Ed:

Diabetes: Oral administration of cinnamon oil was found to significantly reduce blood glucose levels in diabetic KK-Ay mice (Ping et al., 2010)

High Blood Pressure: Cinnamon bark methanol extract showed an acute anti-hypertensive effect on induced hypertensive rates (Nyadjeu et al., 2013)

CLOVE

Steam distillation from bud and stem.

• Powerful antioxidant properties • Promotes circulation • Supports cardiovascular health • Helps soothe teeth and gums • Promotes oral health • Supports a healthy immune system • Powerful for regaining emotional strength * Numbing *

Clove's numbing power makes it a great choice for feeling calm, sore shrapnel sites, achy teeth, achy joints. One drop of ***Clove*** oil has an antioxidant capacity of over 1 million! The highest of any food.

Additional Research from Modern Essentials Book, 6th Ed:

Blood Clots: Clove oil demonstrated an ability to prevent the aggregation of platelets that can lead to blood clots and thrombosis both in vivo and in vitro (Saeed et al., 1994)

CAUTION: Since this oil can prevent the blood platelets from clogging, please talk to your doctor if you are on Warfarin, anti-depressants, Pethidine, seratonin reuptake inhibitors, indirect sympathomimetric drugs.

CYPRESS

Steam distilled from needles, cones, twigs.

Our ***Cypress*** comes from an island off the coast of Greece called Crete.

• Assists with clear breathing • Promotes healthy respiratory function • Soothes tight, tense muscles • Supports localized blood flow • Beneficial for oily skin conditions

Cypress is very helpful in making things flow again: be it emotions, or blood or toxins. Great for draining lymph glands during lymphatic drain therapy. Really helps with bone spurs and carpal tunnel.

►Use on scars and shrapnel sites, bone spur sites. Be consistent with it.

►Use to help life flow again! Use topically one drop on each foot sometime during the day.

►Use on temples, one drop, or along with one drop Frankincense for calming and release. Especially during onset of anxious events.

DEEP SOOTHING BLEND

Various distillation.

• Soothes sore muscles and achy joints • Supports healthy circulation

This is a must-have for achy parts! It is a blend of ***Wintergreen, Camphor, Peppermint, Blue Tansy, German Chamomile, Helichrysum, Osmanthus.***

All of these oils have multiple benefits for soothing the body. It comes in a drop form or a Rubbing Cream. If you get the cream, be sure to layer on oils before the cream. For example: I'm going to use 3 drops ***Peppermint,*** then the ***Deep Soothing Rubbing Cream*** over the top. MMMMM, feels great!

►Rub pea-sized dab of Rubbing Cream and smooth over sore areas. If you want a stronger effect, smear it on like buttering toast and leave on top of skin. For lesser effect rub in.

DETOXIFICATION OIL BLEND

New and Improved formulation now includes CILANTRO!

• **Tangerine Peel :** extremely rich in limonene, known for its purifying benefits • ***Rosemary*** **Flower/Leaf:** supports healthy liver function • **Geranium Plant:** supports the body's natural ability to rid itself of unwanted substances • ***Juniper Berry*****:** supports healthy kidney function • **Cilantro Leaf:** supports the body's natural process of eliminating toxins

Detoxification Softgels: Same as the oil blend in an easy-to-take softgel for internal use instead of manually filling capsules with oil.

Detoxification Complex Capsules:

• Supports healthy cleansing and filtering functions of the liver, kidneys, colon, lungs, and skin

• Supports normal self-detoxification functions of the cleansing organs

Psyllium (Plantago ovata) husk, Rhubarb (Rheum pamatum root), Barberry (Berberis Vulgaris) root and bark, Kelp (Ascophyllum and Laminaria), Milk Thistle (Silybum marianum) seed extract, Safflower (Carthamus tinctorius) flower, Acasia (Acacia Senegal) gum, Osha (Ligusticum porteri) root, Marshmallow (Althaea officinalis) root, Dandelion (Taraxacum officinale) root extract, Garlic (Allium sativum) bulb, Red Clover (Trifolium pratense) flowering tops, Burdock (Arctium lappa) root extract, Clove (Syzgium aromaticum) buds, Amylase, Cellulase, Magnesium yeast, Manganese yeast, in veggie cap.

► Use oil form on bottoms of feet once or twice per day, 2 drops massaged in each foot.

► Take capsules or softgels as directed on container.

DIGESTIVE BLEND

Various distillations

• Aids in the digestion of foods • Soothes occasional stomach upset • Maintains a healthy gastrointestinal tract

This is a blend of ***Ginger, Peppermint, Tarragon, Fennel, Caraway, Coriander, Anise***.

Super good for stomach discomfort, and overeating. Helps with diarrhea AND constipation! Calms nausea.

CAUTION: Not for use by persons with epilepsy; talk to your doctor.

► Use 2 drops under the tongue, or apply them directly on stomach.

EUCALYPTUS

Steam distillation from leaves

• Assists with clear breathing • Supports overall respiratory health • Soothes tired, sore muscles • Purifies and cleanses • Helps to lessen stress • Promotes oral health • Supports healthy immune system function **Super good for breathing!

Additional Research from Modern Essentials Book, 6th Ed:

Analgesic properties: 1,8 cineole (eucalyptus) was found to have antinociceptive (pain-reducing) properties similar to morphine (Liapi et al., 2007)

High blood pressure: Treatment of rats with 1,8 cineole (eucalyptol, found in eucalyptus and rosemary) demonstrated an ability to lower mean aortic pressure (blood pressure), without decreasing heart rate, through vascular wall relaxation (Lahlou et al., 2002)

FENNEL

Steam distillation from crushed seeds

• Relieves occasional indigestion and digestive troubles • Eases monthly menstrual cycles • Supports a healthy lymphatic system • Calms minor skin irritation

This oil tastes great just under the tongue! Really helps with nausea.

Additional Research from Modern Essentials Book, 6th Ed:

Cells: Oral pretreatment with fennel essential oil was found to inhibit in vivo genotoxicity of cyclophosophamide (an important chemotherapy medication with adverse effects) in mouse bone marrow and sperm. These findings suggest that fennel could be used as an adjuvant in chemotherapeutic applications to help diminish adverse effects (Tripathi et al., 2013)

TRIVIA: Ancient Egyptians and Romans awarded garlands of fennel as praise to victorious warriors because fennel was believed to bestow strength, courage, and longevity. It has been used for thousands of years for snakebites, to stave off hunger pains, to tone the female reproductive system, for earaches, eye problems, insect bites, kidney complaints, lung imbalances, and to expel worms.

FOCUS BLEND

Various distillation

• Eases muscle tension in the head and neck • Helps reduce tension, stress, and worry • Soothes the mind and body • Calms emotions

This is a blend of ***Amyris, Patchouli, Frankincense, Lime, Ylang-Ylang, Sandalwood, Roman Chamomile.*** Really helps with clarity and focus, hyper feelings, and stress.

►Simply roll this on the forehead, or neck, or brain stem! So easy to use in a 10 ml roller bottle.

FRACTIONATED COCONUT OIL: Fractionated coconut oil is a fraction of the coconut oil from which almost all the long chain triglycerides are removed, thus leaving mainly the medium-chain triglycerides and making it an absolutely saturated oil(liquid). This saturation gives it a very, very long shelf life and greatly increased stability. In addition, fractionating raises the comparative concentration of capric acid and caprylic acid, thus giving it more of antioxidant and disinfecting effect.

FRANKINCENSE ~ *King of Oils*

Steam distillation from the resin or 'tears' of trees

• Helps build and maintain a healthy immune system • Promotes cellular health • Reduces the appearance of blemishes and rejuvenates skin • Supports healthy immune system function • Promotes feelings of peace, relaxation, satisfaction, and overall wellness.

Perhaps the most precious of the ancient oils, ***Frankincense*** is highly sought after by modern consumers for its many uses including relaxation, immune support, and mood enhancement. This oil is often called "Liquid Gold"; the most versatile oil in your arsenal of Warrior Essential Oils. When you don't know what to use, grab Frankincense. It supports anything and everything in the body. My daughter uses it to ward off seizures from TBI. (Always work with your physician on this) and for skin & scars, and to improve mood. It eases hyper, irritable, agitated, impatient feelings. It is good at assisting the body at reducing inflamed areas of the body. It helps the body regenerate itself. It's a Monoterpene which stimulates apoptosis (helps body remove dead cells, which otherwise could accumulate into tumors).

Barry Jacobs, Phd, Princeton University, said, "Stress is the most important precipitator of depression." ***Frankincense*** really helps alleviate depression, and facilitates spiritual growth.

►Use 2 drops under tongue before rising out of bed. Use another 2 drops after 3:00 pm. You may want to use more if needed. It's very hard to have too much, but because of expense, just start with this.

►Apply one drop on scarred areas of skin. Use 1-2X a day

►Inhale from bottle during emotional work when you want to have more clarity. Or diffuse in diffuser.

►Combine one drop ***Frankincense*** and one drop ***Peppermint*** on hand, rub together, cup over nose and inhale for super clarity and focus. Best to do at "lull" times of day, like at work after you eat lunch.

►Use daily for best results!!

Additional Research from Modern Essentials Book, 6th Ed:

An extract from ***Frankincense*** was found to produce apoptosis in human leukemia cells (Bhushan et al., 2007)

ß-elemene-a sesquiterpene found in curcumin and Boswellia frereana (frankincense) and black pepper essential oils-is currently being studied for its promising potential to induce apoptosis and inhibit cancer cell proliferation in ovarian (Zou et al, 2013), liver (Dai et al, 2013), breast (Zhang et al, 2013, Ding et al., 2013), bladder (Li et al, 2013), lung (Li et al., 2013, Chen et al., 2012), and brain (Li et al., 2012) cancer cell lines, both on its own and in combination with cisplatin chemotherapy.

TRIVIA: The Frankincense trail in the Middle East is so well-worn over the centuries, that it can be seen from outer space.

These statements have not been evaluated by the Food and Drug Administration. This product is not intended to diagnose, treat, cure, or prevent any disease.

GERANIUM~for Worry & Stress***

Steam distillation from leaves

• Promotes clear, healthy skin • Helps calm nerves and lessen stress *Supports liver health

Everything about this oil is soothing to the senses. It has a sweet, green, citrus-rose fresh scent. ***Geranium*** has a way of "opening up the creative side of the brain" bringing about clarity and calmness, and creativity to life situations. It makes us more able to problem-solve, because the right side of the brain opens up to creative solutions. Its smell is distinctive and peaceful. It has a way of overtaking the senses and helps shift the mood. It can be habit-forming; in a good way ☺

It's also superb for mixing with liquid facial cleanser to promote clear skin.

►Use by itself or with ***Frankincense*** when doing emotional~breathing work. Put 1 drop of each in hands, rub together and cup over nose to inhale. Rub on brain stem.

►Massage 1 drop on bottom of each foot. Inhale from bottle, or diffuse in occupied areas.

►Apply 1 drop on each wrist for relaxation.

► Anxiety Inhalant: Put 2 drops ***Geranium***, 2 drops ***Ylang Ylang***, 3 drops ***Frankincense***, 1 drop ***Vetiver*** on hands. Rub together and cup over nose and inhale.

► ***Geranium*** Tea: A few drops in honey or agave then add hot water (not boiling) will soothe diarrhea and slow or stop internal bleeding.

►Use 1 drop on washrag with your regular soap for facial wash, or body wash. Make sure you do the skin test on inside of elbow to check for sensitivity.

Additional Research from Modern Essentials Book, 6th Ed:

A formulation of lemongrass and geranium oil was found to reduce airborne bacteria by 89% in an office environment after diffusion for 15 hours (Doran et al., 2009)

*****CAUTION: Geranium oil can lower your blood sugar level. Use it (internally) with caution if you have hypoglycemia or low blood sugar.**

GRAPEFRUIT

Cold-pressed from rind

• Cleanses and purifies • Beneficial for oily skin issues • Supports healthy metabolism • Helps reduce mental and physical fatigue • Helps with sore muscles and joints

This oil is uplifting and good for detoxification. It supports healthy lymph glands.

►Diffuse in occupied areas for depression.

►Put 4 drops in a veggie cap and take internally.

►Use caution when applying topically, as any citrus causes photo-sensitivity with sunshine. Can cause skin burn.

Smelling grapefruit floating around the house from the diffuser is a special experience. Since this fruity oil is expressed from the rind, it may not interfere with medication, but speak with your doctor before taking internally if you are on beta blockers.

Additional Research from Modern Essentials Book, 6th Ed:

Obesity: Grapefruit essential oil was found to directly inhibit adipogenesis of adipocytes, indicating that grapefruit has an anti-obesity effect (Haze et al., 2010)

GROUNDING BLEND

Various distillations

Spruce, Ho Wood, Blue Tansy, Frankincense, German Chamomile, Fractionated Coconut oil

• Creates a sense of calm and well-being • Promotes whole-body relaxation • Brings harmony to the mind and body • Soothes sore muscles and joints

It has a comforting unique smell, very pleasant to the senses, kind of foresty, and light.

►Use 2 drops massaged into bottoms of feet or along spine in morning.

►Can be used in navel. Can be used NEAT. (no dilution except if someone has known skin sensitivity)

►Diffuse in occupied areas for scattered feelings.

HELICHRYSUM

• Helps skin recover quickly • Promotes healthy liver function • Supports localized blood flow • Help detoxify the body • Promote circulation • Helps reduce the appearance of wrinkles and other blemishes • Promotes a glowing, youthful complexion • Helps relieve tension

This oil is indispensable for warriors. It's regenerative properties support anger management, and feelings of a broken heart. It also helps with dizziness, sciatic pain, bloody noses, tooth abscess and much more.

Our ***Helichrysum*** is harvested by hand in the high elevation hillsides of Indian mountains, and brought down steep trails from its native habitat. It is painstakingly distilled from flowers at just the right time to ensure peak potency and purity!

►Apply 1 drop around outer ear for ringing.

►Use on skin for rejuvenating.

►Put a drop on the heart chakra for feeling wounded.

<u>Additional Research from Modern Essentials Book, 6th Ed:</u>

Arzanol (extracted from helichrysum) inhibited HIV-1 replication in T-cells and also inhibited the release of pro-inflammatory cytokines (chemical messengers) in monocytes (Appendino et al., 2007)

INVIGORATING BLEND

Various distillation methods from citrus rinds

• Cleanses and purifies the air and surfaces • Helps reduce stress and uplift mood • Positively affects mood with energizing and refreshing properties

This is a blend of ***Orange, Lemon, Grapefruit, Mandarin, Bergamot, Tangerine, Clementine, Vanilla Bean extract***. It smells like the old-fashioned Orange-Sicles you used to get as a kid! It is very UPLIFTING to mood, and all the guys love this one.

►Diffuse, diffuse, diffuse!! Use this in occupied areas for depression. Keep it going 24/7

JOYFUL BLEND~Contains Melissa!

This blend consists of: ***Lavandin, Tangerine, Elemi, Lemon Myrtle, Melissa, Ylang Ylang, Osmanthus, Sandalwood.***

Very comforting in diffuser. Uplifting scent, live particles (of course! All the oils are alive!) create harmony in mood, and cleanse the air of threats and bad vibes! Helps dispel ANGER and Depression.

►DIFFUSE this oil often and inhale straight from the bottle!

CAUTION:** Can make skin photosensitive for 12 hours to direct sunlight!

LAVENDER

Steam distilled from flowering top

• Widely used for its calming and relaxing qualities • Soothes occasional skin irritations • Helps skin recover quickly • Eases muscle tension

This oil is part of the FLiP TRINITY of OILS: ***Frankincense, Lavender and Peppermint.*** It has a major calming effect for any anxious situations. My daughter keeps some at her bedside, and in the glovebox for driving. She also bathes in it before bed. Can be sensually enhancing.

►Massage 1 drop around outer ear if awakened with nightmare.

►Diffuse in occupied rooms when anxiety levels are peaking or there is nagging depression.

►Can be used in recipes like cakes and cookies. Can be applied NEAT (no dilution) but always use care as they are very concentrated molecules ☺

Additional Research from Modern Essentials Book, 6th Ed:

Anxiety - Patients waiting for dental treatment were found to be less anxious and have a better mood when exposed to the odor of lavender or orange oil compared to control (Lehrner et al., 2005)

Anxiety and Sleep - A study with 56 percutaneous coronary intervention patients in an intensive care unit found that an aromatherapy blend of lavender, Roman Chamomile, and neroli decreased anxiety and improved sleep quality when compared to conventional nursing intervention (Cho et al., 2013)

LEMON

Cold-pressed from rind (requires 3,000 lemons to produce a kilo of oil)

• Cleanses and purifies the air and surfaces • Naturally cleanses the body and aids in digestion • Supports healthy respiratory function • Promotes a positive mood and cognitive ability • Helps ward off free radicals with its antioxidant benefits • Soothes an irritated throat

Avoid sunlight** for 12 hours on areas where citrus oils are used topically.

Lemon water should be drank a few times a day for supporting cleansing in the body. Always use glass containers for citrus oils.

►Put 2 drops on spine for mental focus and calming.

►Diffuse in occupied areas.

►Drink in ice water, 2-3 drops depending on liking, throughout the day for refreshing.

Additional Research from Modern Essentials Book, 6th Ed:

Anti-depressent properties: Lemon oil and its component, citral, were found to decrease depressed behavior in rats involved in several stress tests in a manner similar to antidepressant drugs (Komori et al., 1995)

Anti-cancer properties: In a study of older individuals, it was found that there was a dose-dependent relationship between citrus peel consumption (which are high in d-Limonene) and a lower degree of squamous cell carcinoma (SCC) of the skin (Hakim et al., 2000)

MARJORAM

Steam distilled from leaves

• Valued for its calming properties and positive effect on the nervous system • Soothes tired, stressed muscles • Supports a healthy respiratory system • Benefits the cardiovascular system • Promotes gastrointestinal health • Purifies the skin

This one is super good for nerve discomfort, like ligaments, tendons, sciatic.

►Use 1-2 drops along discomfort sites, then layer Wintergreen or Deep Soothing Blend over top.

►To enhance sleep, put 2 drops on bottom of each foot.

Additional Research from Modern Essentials Book, 6th Ed:

High Blood Pressure: Eighty-three hypertensive or pre-hypertensive subjects were divided into the following three groups: a study group, (exposed to an essential oil blend containing lavender, ylang ylang, marjoram, and nerouli), a placebo group (exposed to artificial fragrance), and a control group (no interventions).The study group was found to have an immediate and long-term decrease in high blood pressure (Kim et al., 2012)

MELALEUCA

Steam distillation from leaves

• Renowned for its cleansing and rejuvenating effect on the skin • Promotes healthy immune function* • Protects against environmental and seasonal threats*

►For occasional skin irritations apply 1-2 drops onto affected area.

►Add 1-2 drops to water, citrus drinks, or veggie caps to support healthy immune system function.*

►Combine 1-2 drops with your facial cleanser or moisturizer for added cleansing properties.

►Apply to skin after shaving.

►Apply to fingernails and toenails after showering to purify and keep nails looking healthy.

There are so many wonderful uses for this versatile oil, that proper attention should be given to it, and more information and scientific studies can be found in the *Modern Essential Book 7th Edition.* This can be purchased at Aromatools.com for about $27.00 plus shipping and handling. Very well worth the money if you are serious about essential oils. OR, you can look on pubmed.com for extensive scientific research on essential oils.

MELISSA ~ *(Lemon Balm)*

Steam distilled from leaves and flowers

• Supports and helps boost a healthy immune system • Calms tension and nerves • Addresses occasional stomach discomfort • Helps initiate a restful sleep • Promotes emotional and cognitive health *Light lemony scent

"***Melissa*** is the nearest one can find to a rejuvenator....[it] helps to cushion the effects of our mind and the world outside on our body." *-Modern Essentials, 6th Ed*

Dr. Dietrich Wabner, a professor at the Technical University of Munich, reported that a one time application of true Melissa oil led to complete remission of herpes simplex lesions. *- Modern Essentials, 6th Ed*

►Diffuse this oil, or inhale. Also, can be applied with little or no dilution. This is a plant that can be easily grown in your garden, or a pot. I have grown it, and it's very low maintenance. Keep in mind, the oil is super concentrated and you will need a LOT of the plant to equal one drop of Melissa oil.

►***Respiratory Drops*** contain ***Melissa***, and are super effective for calming! And they are easy to slip into your purse or pocket.

►*Joyful Blend* also contains ***Melissa*** oil. Diffuse it liberally for angriness and frustration. Apply 2 drops to brain stem as needed for agitated and anxious feelings.

►The pure oil is suggested, however, for maximum benefits. Try to obtain the purest ***Melissa*** oil you can.

►Apply 1 drop to bottom of each foot as needed. The feet absorb oils very quickly and efficiently.

Additional Research from Modern Essentials Book, 6th Ed:

Melissa oil demonstrated inhibition of Herpes simplex type 1 and 2 viruses. (Schnitzler et al., 2008)

Sedative properties: Results of a clinical trial indicate that a combination of melissa and valerian oils may have anxiety-reducing properties at some doses (Kennedy et al., 2006)

AND....***Melissa*** (lemon Balm) oil applied topically in a lotion was found to reduce agitation and to improve quality of life factors in patients suffering severe dementia compared to those receiving a placebo lotion (Ballard et al., 2002)

MYRRH

Steam distillation from gum resin

• Powerful cleansing properties, especially for the mouth and throat • Soothes the skin; promotes a smooth, youthful-looking complexion • Promotes emotional balance and well-being *Similar to Frankincense in effect, but more of an earthy-smell.

Myrrh is very comforting. It is thick and rich, and stays with you for a while, supporting you through trials. This oil can be used NEAT (no dilution), and it's wonderful to put a couple drops on your fingers and massage into your face! You can use it anywhere on your body where you need support or are 'afraid' of a problem existing. It is super thick to get out of bottle, and you may need to remove lid. The way you can tell that you have really good ***Myrrh***, is it will tend to form 'crusties' around top after it's been open a while. This is because the Myrrh is trying to go back to being a gum resin when it's exposed to the air. If your oil does not do this, it may not be as effective. ☺

►Use 1-2 drops on skin for emotional support and skin issues.

►Inhale when feeling triggered or afraid.

►Great for foot fungus issues, skin issues, flaky skin, itchy skin. Ok for outer genitalia. Always try a little diluted first.

►Enjoy the exotic richness of this oil!

PATCHOULI

Mint Family

Steam distilled from leaves

• Promotes a smooth, glowing complexion • Recognized for its musky-sweet aroma

This oil is one of the "Blood Brain Barrier" oils. If you can stand the smell, it's a super supporter of the brain. It is 63% sesquiterpenes. Search pbmed.gov for scientific studies.

►Add to daily moisturizer to help reduce the appearance of blemishes.

►Add three to four drops in a diffuser to help provide grounding and balance emotions.

►Apply one to two drops to back of neck after a long day of work.

►Put one drop of ***Patchouli***, one drop ***Bergamot*** in hands and rub together. Cup over nose and inhale for balancing emotions. Diffuse together in occupied areas..

►Place a drop in belly button for grounding effect. Dab on wrists when bloated. DO NOT put it under the tongue as the properties in it will dry your mouth out.

PEPPERMINT

Steamed distilled from leaves

• Promotes healthy respiratory function and clear breathing • Alleviates occasional stomach upset • Frequently used in toothpaste and chewing gum for oral health

*Cooling ***Peppermint*** is part of FLiP Trinity of Oils. ***Peppermint*** has a super~cooling effect for head discomfort; apply preemptively at onset of rage, and after rage. It is very strong. One drop = 28 cups of Peppermint tea, so start with one drop!

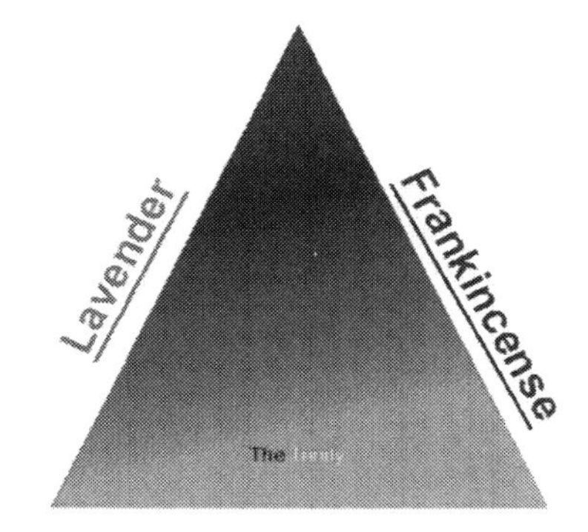

Additional Research from Modern Essentials Book, 6th Ed:

Mice pre-treated with an injection of peppermint essential oil demonstrated no seizures and 100% post-treatment survival after being injected with a lethal dose of pentylenetetrazol (PTZ) to cause seizures (Koutroumaidou et al., 2013)

A combination of peppermint oil and ethanol was found to have a significant analgesic effect with a reduction in sensitivity to headache; while a combination of peppermint, eucalyptus, and ethonol was found to relax muscles and to increase cognitive performance in humans (Göbel et al., 1994)

TRIVIA: The finest Peppermint in the world grows in our home state of Washington in the Pacific Northwest!

PROTECTIVE BLEND

Various distillations

• Supports healthy immune function • Protects against environmental threats • Cleans surfaces • Purifies the skin while promoting healthy circulation • Energizing, uplifting aroma

A blend of ***Orange, Clove Bud, Cinnamon Bark, Eucalyptus, Rosemary.*** It has a wonderful spicy scent, and keeps at bay many environmental threats.

►Diffuse in occupied areas.

►Put 1 drop on bottoms of feet morning and evening.

►Use 1 drop on toothbrush when brushing teeth.

►Use 5 drops in misting glass bottle for cleaning surfaces

TRIVIA: This is a blend from ancient times, that the perfumers developed in the Middle Ages, to protect themselves when robbing the graves of dead persons who had been thrown into mass graves due to the Black Plague. They were able to avoid contracting the disease by using it.

RESPIRATORY BLEND with Cardamon

• Maintains clear airways and breathing • Supports overall respiratory health • Helps minimize the effects of seasonal threats

Blend of ***Laurel Leaf, Peppermint, Eucalyptus, Melaleuca, Lemon, Ravensara, Cardamom.***

Can't live without this one for anxiety, panic, and good breathing in general!

►Massage 1 drop on chest for seasonal or environmental threats.

►Put 1 drop on backs of hands or wrists.

►Excellent for diffusing around the house and at bedtime for curbing snoring!

RESPIRATORY DROPS with Melissa!

• Maintains clear airways and breathing • Supports overall respiratory health • Calms the senses • Supports mental clarity and function

These drops are made of: Organic Evaporated Cane Juice, Organic Brown Rice Syrup, ***Lemon Essential Oil, Peppermint Essential Oil, Cardamom Essential Oil, Eucalyptus Essential Oil, Thyme Essential Oil, Melissa Essential Oil.*** They really do the trick for agitation, anxiety, respiratory health for us.

►Use a throat drop in a cup of your favorite tea~listen to it crackle as it melts to release all the goodness and aromatic benefits. So soothing!

►Use a drop whenever stressed or having environmental threats.

ROSEMARY

Steam distilled from flowering plant

• Supports healthy digestion • Soothes sore muscles and joints • Helps reduce nervous tension and fatigue

This oil is thought to support hair growth. It is rejuvenating to stalling adrenals. Has many of the same benefits of Basil.

Blends with: ***Basil, Frankincense, Lavender, Peppermint, Eucalyptus, and Marjoram***.

Additional Research from Modern Essentials Book, 6th Ed:

Blood Pressure-Low: Oral treatment with rosemary essential oil on primary hypotensive subjects was found to increase blood pressure values when compared to the subjects' placebo treatments before and after rosemary treatment (Fernandez et al., 2014)

Analgesic properties: An ethanol extract of rosemary was found to demostrate antinociceptive (pain-blocking) and anti-inflammatory activity in mice and rats (Gonzalez-Trujano et al., 2007)

►**CAUTION:** not for use in persons with EPILEPSY. Also may increase blood pressure. Consult your doctor.

SOUL SUPPORT COLLECTION OF OILS

A collection of six blends to support the soul:

COMFORTING BLEND

Frankincense Resin, Patchouli Leaf, Ylang Ylang Flower, Labdanum Leaf/Stalk, Amyris Bark, Sandalwood Wood, Rose Flower, Osmanthus Flower

Losing something or someone you love can be deeply disorienting and painful. Words unspoken and questions unanswered may keep you worried and unsettled. The ***Comforting Blend*** of floral and tree essential oils will help you close the door on sadness and take your first steps on a hopeful path to emotional healing. Bind your broken heart.

►Diffuse during times of loss to comfort the soul and evoke feelings of hope.

►Apply over the heart morning and night as a reminder to be patient with healing and to think positive thoughts. (Be careful if skin is sensitive. Use Fractionated Coconut Oil to dilute!)

►Apply 1-2 drops to a shirt collar or scarf and smell through the day to ward off feelings of grief and sadness.

►Diffuse in occupied areas until mood lifts.

►Topical use: Apply 1-2 drops to desired area. Dilute with Fractionated Coconut oil to minimize any skin sensitivity. See additional precautions.

ENCOURAGING BLEND

Peppermint Plant, Clementine Peel, Coriander Seed, Basil Herb, Yuzu Peel, Melissa Leaf, Rosemary Leaf, Vanilla Bean.

Do you have setbacks that have shaken your confidence in spite of your best efforts? Or has misplaced trust left you cynical more often than your best self should be? Then stop, reset, and restart with this ***Encouraging Blend*** of mint and citrus essential oils. It helps you unleash your creative powers and find the courage that comes from believing in yourself again. Go ahead and raise the bar—you can do it!

►Apply to shirt collar before giving a speech to instill feelings of confidence.

►Apply to pulse points before participating in sporting events or other competitions.

►Diffuse when working on a work or school project to stay motivated.

INSPIRING BLEND

Fractionated Coconut Oil, Cardamom Seed, Cinnamon Bark, Ginger Rhizome, Clove Bud, Sandalwood Wood, Jasmine Flower, Vanilla Bean, Damiana Leaf

Have you lost your why, your mojo, your passion? Too much of even a good thing can become predictable and boring over time. This ***Inspiring Blend*** of spice and herb essential oils will help rekindle excitement in your life. Jump out of an airplane, dive into an ocean, or try something really scary like dancing. With this oil you will find the daring to try something new, as well as discover renewed joy for the current blessings in your life.

►Diffuse in the morning to start the day feeling energized and enthusiastic. Diffuse at work to spark creativity, clarity, and wonder.

►Apply to pulse points and heart throughout the day to feel inspired and passionate.

REASSURING BLEND

Vetiver Root, Lavender Flower, Ylang Ylang Flower, Frankincense Resin, Clary Sage Flower, Marjoram Leaf, Labdanum Leaf/Stalk, Spearmint Herb

Are life's anxious moments leaving you feeling overwhelmed and afraid? This ***Reassuring Blend*** of floral and mint essential oils is a positive reminder you don't have to be perfect to find peace. Slow down, take a deep breath, and reconnect with the composed, collected you. Everything turning out fine begins with believing it will—and a few drops of ***Reassuring Blend***.

►Diffuse at night time to promote a calming environment and restful sleep.

►When experiencing anxious feelings, apply one drop to hands, rub together and inhale deeply.

►Diffuse or inhale before taking a test, presenting to a large group, or in times of worry or distress.

RENEWING BLEND

Spruce Leaf, Bergamot Peel, Juniper Berry Fruit, Myrrh Resin, Arborvitae Wood, Nootka Tree Wood, Thyme Leaf, Citronella Herb

Are you carrying a burden that grows heavier with time? Would you be better off just letting it go and facing a future unfettered by anger and guilt? When you are ready to move forward, the ***Renewing Blend*** of tree and herb essential oils will help you discover the liberating action of forgiving, forgetting, and moving on. Start each of your tomorrows relieved and contented with ***Renewing Blend***.

►Diffuse when meditating to help release harbored feelings of anger and guilt.

►Apply to pulse points and heart throughout the day to feel grounded and content. Have this oil on hand throughout the day to counteract negative emotions that may arise from undesirable situations.

UPLIFTING BLEND

Wild Orange Peel, Clove Bud, Star Anise Fruit/Seed, Lemon Myrtle Leaf, Nutmeg Kernel, Vanilla Bean Extract, Ginger Rhizome, Cinnamon Bark, Zdravetz Herb

Everyone knows a bright disposition and cheerful attitude can smooth over many of the bumps and challenges of life, right? But, sometimes no amount of positive self-talk is enough to avoid the blues. The ***Uplifting Blend*** of citrus and spice essential oils provides a cheerful boost of happiness and positivity when you are feeling down. It's sunshiny, fresh, optimistic aroma will brighten any moment of your day.

►Diffuse at home, work, or school to promote a positive, uplifting environment.

►Apply to a cotton ball, terracotta plate, or just a smooth piece of wood, and place in car to experience ***Uplifting Blend's*** energizing aroma while driving.

►When feeling down, apply one drop to hands, rub together, and inhale deeply as needed throughout the day.

TENSION HEADACHE RELIEF BLEND

Various distillations

• Eases muscle tension in the head and neck • Helps reduce tension, stress, and worry • Soothes the mind and body • Calms emotions

This is highly soothing for head discomfort. It's a blend in a roller bottle of ***Wintergreen, Lavender, Peppermint, Frankincense, Cilantro, Roman chamomile, Marjoram, Basil, Rosemary.*** This is a favorite of my son-in-law's. He uses this at work and keeps it within reach in his work truck.

►Roll on over forehead, back of neck. Use as needed. Fast and effective.

►Keep this in purse or pocket for moderate to severe head discomfort. Pre-emptive use is best, first thing in morning if it's "going to be one of those days".

VETIVER

Steam distilled from roots

• Supports healthy circulation • Calming, grounding effect on emotions • Immune-enhancing properties • Super grounding effect for triggers or feeling 'out-of-body'

What can we say? ***Vetiver*** is the #1 choice for triggers! This is such a great oil for easing feelings of trauma and confusion and shock. Has rich, woody, earthy, smoky undertones of scent. Since ***Vetiver*** is so thick, it's easier to use if you purchase a dropper designed for the 15 ml bottles. Go here:

https://www.aromatools.com/Dropper_Cap_Assembly_for_15_ml_Glass_Vials_p/9157f.htm

Vetiver has a real 'grounding' effect, maybe because it is distilled from a ROOT system.

It has an 'earthy-smell' to it, kind of like you are walking through a huge forest, taking in the earth beneath your feet. At first you may not care for its odor, but please have it on hand at all times.

►Put a drop on backs of hands. Inhale from bottle, or diffuse.

►Cup hands over nose and inhale. This will 'bring you back' right away. You may want to experiment on which oil is right for you when triggered. The sooner the better in using your oils at this time.

WINTERGREEN

Steam distillation from leaves

Wintergreen essential oil is derived from the leaves of a creeping shrub found in coniferous areas. The main chemical component in ***Wintergreen,*** methyl salicylate, is used in topical creams and massage blends because of its soothing properties. In fact, ***Wintergreen*** and ***Birch*** are the only plants in the world that contain methyl salicylate naturally.

As a flavoring, small amounts of ***Wintergreen*** are used in candies, toothpaste, and chewing gum. When diffused, ***Wintergreen*** has a refreshing aroma that's uplifting and stimulating. Our new source of ***Wintergreen*** comes from Nepal, where it is wild harvested by rural villagers, then distilled by community-owned distillation facilities. This process creates increased economic opportunity for very remote regions in rural Nepal.

►Use this oil topically as a layer for soothing discomfort.

WOMEN'S MONTHLY BLEND

Various distillation methods

Rich blend of ***Clary Sage*** (helps hormones), ***Lavender*** (Calming), ***Bergamot*** (uplifting for mood), ***Roman Chamomile*** (gentle soothing), ***Cedarwood*** (soothing to nerves), ***Ylang Ylang*** (calming and sedative), ***Geranium*** (calming), ***Fennel*** (hormone balancing properties), Carrot Seed (soothing to uterus), Palarosa (stress reducer), Vitex (hormone regulating).

Don't you just hate it when someone points out that your irritability could be "your time of the month"? And this gets used as a blame-tactic?? Well, rest assured, this blend will work if it is, or if it isn't! ☺ and it is often mistaken for fine perfume! It comes in a purse-size 10oz roller bottle making it easy to apply whenever and wherever. Great for hot-flashes too.

► Roll it on during or after flashbacks

► Apply to chest, abdomen, or back of neck as needed.

► Diffuse in occupied areas.

YLANG YLANG ~ Sensuality

Steam distilled from flowers

• Helps balance hormones • Promotes healthy skin and hair • Lifts mood while having a calming effect • Helps to lessen tension and stress • Promotes a positive outlook

Ylang Ylang is the oil of sensual influence. It enhances relationships and alleviates anger. It also has many other benefits, like soothing high blood pressure. (talk to your doctor) It's very soothing to emotions, often facilitating Inner Child work. YY is great to put over your heart after emotional shock, or for discomfort in the chest, helping ease one into regular breathing, alleviating irritability. YY helps in connecting spiritually with Divine Mind through your own soul. It softens the harshness of the world, by assuring the Self that its okay to feel the emotions of happiness.

YY is credited with being the oil of eroticism, and newlywed passion.

►Gently massage over heart, or have partner massage in. Can be used during a massage table technique, or massaged on ears before intimacy.

►Inhale deeply during times of stress and agitation.

Companion oils: Calming Blend, Orange, Geranium, Vetiver, Sandalwood, Marjoram, Grapefruit, Lemon

TRIVIA: Ylang Ylang has been used to cover the beds of newlywed couples on their wedding night. ♥

These statements have not been evaluated by the Food and Drug Administration. This product is not intended to diagnose, treat, cure, or prevent any disease.

APPENDIX 2
Possible Drug Interactions

Table 1: Possible Drug Interactions with Essential Oils

Drugs	Essential Oils (EO)	Route of EO Administration	Possible Interactions
Warfarin (anticoagulant)	Birch, wintergreen	All (Topical, Aromatic, Internal)	Inhibits platelet adhesion and intensifies blood thinning
CYP2B6 (liver metabolizing enzyme) substrates	Melissa	Internal	Inhibits CYP2B6, which could enhance drug action
	Lemongrass	All (Topical, Aromatic, Internal)	
Aspirin (antiplatelet) Heparin (anticoagulant) Warfarin (anticoagulant)	Birch, cassia, cinnamon, clove, fennel (sweet), marjoram, oregano, patchouli, thyme, wintergreen	Internal	Inhibits platelet adhesion and intensifies blood thinning
Monoamine oxidase inhibiting antidepressants (including isocarboxazid, moclobemide, phenelzine, selegiline, tranylcypromine)	Clove	Internal	Clove oil constituents inhibit monoamine oxidase enzymes, which could affect blood pressure and cause tremors or confusion
Pethidine (opioid analgesic)	Clove	Internal	Increase of serotonin, which could cause agitation, delirium, headache, convulsions, and/or hyperthermia
Selective serotonin reuptake inhibitors (including citalopram escitalopram, fluoxetine, paroxetine, sertraline)	Clove	Internal	Increase of brain serotonin levels, which could cause vomiting, nausea, increased body temperature, hallucinations, etc.
Indirect sympathomimetic drugs (including ephedrine, amphetamine)	Clove	Internal	Possible hypertension, increased heart rate, and arrhythmias
Antidiabetic drugs (including glibenclamide, tolbutamide, metformin)	Cassia, cinnamon, dill, fennel (sweet), lemongrass, marjoram, melissa, oregano	Internal	Constituents of these oils influence blood sugar levels and may cause hyperglycemia or hypoglycemia
Dermal medications (including drug patches) Use caution with all essential oils Topical Essential oils can enhance skin absorption of drugs and increase blood plasma levels, resulting in a delivered dose higher than needed	Use caution with all essential oils	Topical	Essential oils can enhance skin absorption of drugs and increase blood plasma levels, resulting in a delivered dose higher than needed

The above information was adapted from Essential Oil Safety by Robert Tisserand and Rodney Young (2014, p. 58-59). Only essential oils included in the Single Essential Oils section of this book are listed in this table. Other essential oils not included in this book may produce similar drug interactions.

Common Drugs Originating from Plants		
Plant-Based Drug	**Medicinal Use**	**Plant Connection**
Aspirin	Painkiller, anti-inflammatory, and fever reducer	Aspirin is a synthetic derivative of the natural compound salicylic acid. Salicylic acid can be found in the bark of the willow tree and other plants (including cucumbers and potatoes).
Atropine	Anesthetic and anticholinergic agent (used for the treatment of extremely low heart rate [bradycardia])	Atropine is a secondary metabolite found in plants of the family Solanaceae, including nightshade, Jimson weed, and mandrake.
Digoxin	Various heart conditions (i.e. heart failure and irregular heartbeat)	Digoxin contains chemicals taken from foxglove plants.
Ephedrine	Asthma, hay fever, and colds	Ephedrine is a chemical found in plants in the genus *Ephedra*.
Morphine	Relieves intense pain	Morphine can be found in the unripe seedpods of opium poppy plants.
Paclitaxel	Treatment of solid tumor cancers	Paclitaxel is isolated from the bark of the Pacific yew.
Pilocarpine	Dry mouth and glaucoma	Pilocarpine is a chemical harvested from the leaves of tropical American shrubs from the genus Pilocarpus.
Quinine	Malaria	Quinine is found naturally in cinchona tree bark.
Reserpine	Antipsychotic	Reserpine is isolated from the dried root of Indian snake-root.

APPENDIX 3 Affirmations

"I can ask for help without feeling like I'm a burden."

" I have willingness to do whatever it takes to feel like a better version of myself"

"I can be equal to another person in a relationship" ♂♀

"A way will be shown to me."

" It is okay to give myself a break."

"It is okay to ask someone to show me how to do things."

"I am lovable."

"I am worth it."

"It's okay to play and have fun."

"It's okay to know another way to live."

"My feelings are okay even if I'm still learning how to distinguish them."

"I have a right to as much time as I need to experiment with this new information and these new ideas, and to initiate changes in my life."

"It's okay to say I love myself."

"Its okay to think about things differently than others."

"It is okay to have dreams and have hope."

"I have a right to 'mess up,' to make mistakes, to blow it, to disappoint myself, or fall short of the mark."

"I have a right to express my feelings in a non-destructive way and at a safe time and place."

"I have a right to carve out my place in the world."

"I have a right to put an end to conversations with people who make me feel put down and humiliated."

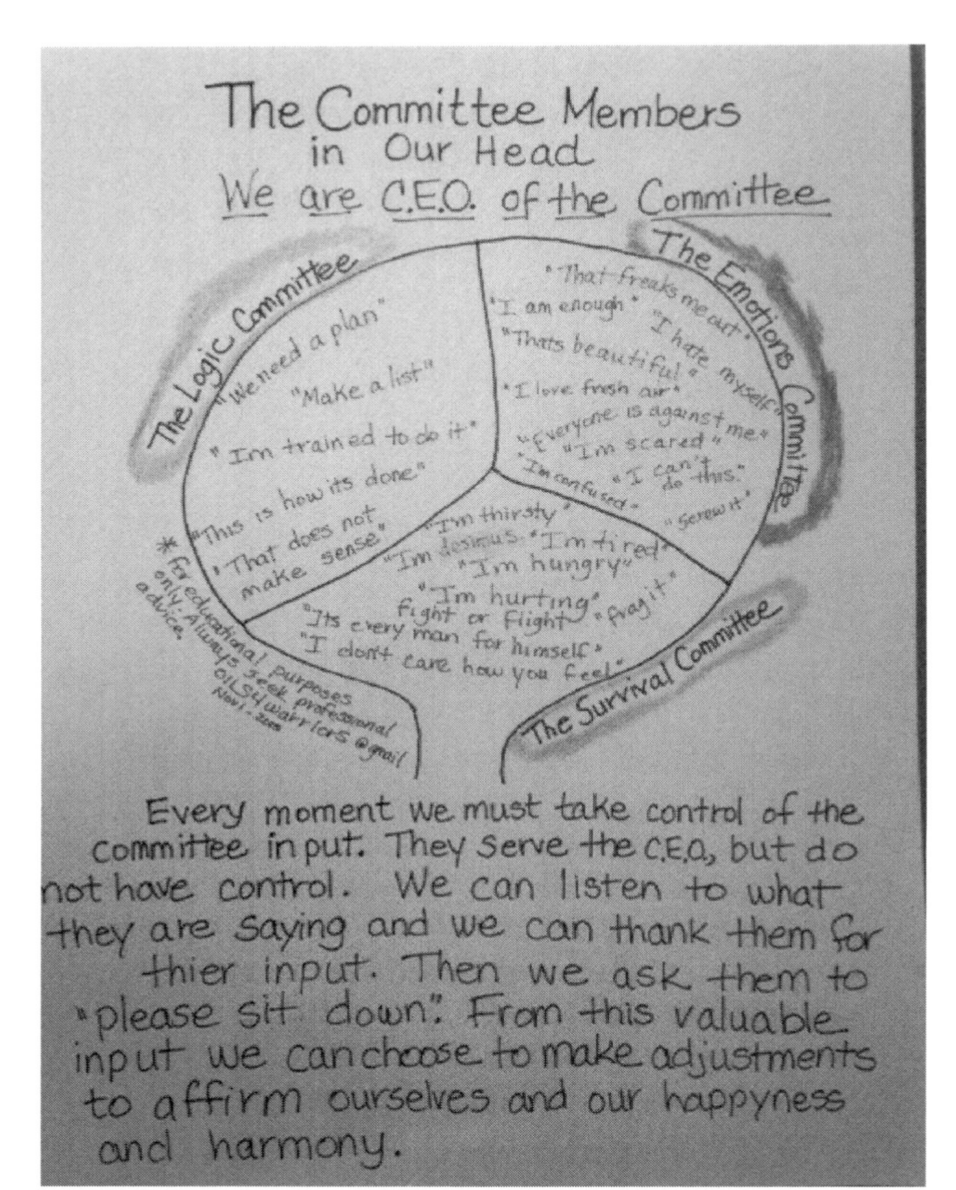
The Committee Members
in Our Head
We are C.E.O. of the Committee
The Logic Committee
"We need a plan"
"Make a list"
"I'm trained to do it"
"This is how its done"
"That does not make sense"
The Emotions Committee
"That freaks me out"
"I am enough"
"I hate myself"
"Thats beautiful"
"I love fresh air"
"Everyone is against me"
"I'm scared"
"I'm confused"
"I can't do this."
"Screw it"
The Survival Committee
"I'm thirsty"
"I'm tired"
"I'm hungry"
"I'm hurting"
fight or flight
"Its every man for himself"
"I don't care how you feel"
* For educational purposes only. Always seek professional advice.
Every moment we must take control of the committee input. They serve the C.E.O, but do not have control. We can listen to what they are saying and we can thank them for thier input. Then we ask them to "please sit down". From this valuable input we can choose to make adjustments to affirm ourselves and our happyness and harmony.

APPENDIX 4 Emotions List

Abandoned
adored
affectionate
afraid
aggressive
alarmed
alert
alienated
amazed
amused
angry
annoyed
antagonistic
anxious
apathetic
apologetic
appreciated
apprehensive
approved of
ashamed
at ease
awed
baffled
brilliant
capable
discontented
disgusted
dissatisfied
eager
ecstatic
edgy
elated
embarrassed
enchanted
enraged
enthusiastic
envious
estranged
exasperated
excited
exhausted
fatigued
fed up
forlorn
friendly
frightened
frustrated
furious
glad
gloomy
jealous
jolly
joyful
lethargic
liked
listless
lonely
loved
mischievous
miserable
mixed up
moody
negative
numb
optimistic
pained
panicky
paranoid
passionate
peaceful
pleased
pressured
proud
provoked
puzzled
timid
tired
torn up
trapped
troubled
turned off
turned on
uncomfortable
undecided
unhappy
unimportant
unloved
unwanted
unpopular
unsure
burden
upset
useless
vengeful
vibrant
victimized
victorious
vigorous
wanted
weak

cautious
comfortable
concerned
confused
content
courageous
curious
cynical
degraded
dejected
delighted
dependent
depressed
despised
determined
detested
disappointed
determined
gratified
hopeless
hopeful
horrified
humiliated
hurt
hysterical
impatient
important
inadequate
independent
indifferent
indignant
infuriated
isolated
innocent
inspired
interested
regretful
rejected
relaxed
relieved
reluctant
resentful
sad
scared
seductive
serene
sheepish
shocked
shy
sick
smart
strong
surprised
suspicious
weary
wicked
wide awake
withdrawn
worn out
worried
worthless
wimpy
wretched
wrong

APPENDIX 5
Possible 12 steps of Combat PTSD Recovery

Just a word about the stigma of 'recovery'....it affects everyone on the planet. Everyone is 'recovering' from one thing or another. With warriors, the effects of a battlefield can become spiritually problematic if one's belief in something like "God" has been abandoned altogether due to cynicism from being through war trauma. A belief in 'Spirit', 'Creator', 'Universe', H.P. (Higher Power), can be almost impossible to envision for some of us. That being said, it's important to entertain the idea of something greater than humanity to restore us. All we are asking is, can you consider it? ~ Love to all.....

1. We recognized that we were powerless over the effects of living in a war zone and that our lives have become unmanageable since leaving it. (sugg. oils: ***Clove, Ginger, Grounding Blend, Reassuring Blend***)
2. We became willing to reconsider that a power greater than ourselves might be able to add more light on our existence. (sugg. Oil: ***Frankincense, Uplifting Blend***)
3. We made a commitment to re-learn how to love ourselves, however troubled we perceive ourselves right now. (sugg. Oils: ***Ginger, Grounding Blend, Cilantro, Encouraging Blend***)
4. We made a courageously honest inventory of the things or people we judged and hated, because in essence, we become like that which we hated. (sugg. Oils: ***Thyme, Calming Blend, Geranium, Cleansing Blend, Cilantro, Reassuring Blend***)

5. We admitted to the Universe, to ourselves, and to another Battle Bud, the exact nature of our actions and how we felt. (sugg. Oils: ***Roman Chamomile, Frankincense, Comforting Blend***)
6. We were ready to begin the healing process with help from G.O.D. (Good Orderly Direction) (sugg. Oil: ***Arborvitae, Encouraging Blend***)
7. We asked The Universe for help in finding our way to heal. (sugg. Oils: ***Geranium, Frankincense, DNA Repair Blend, Encouraging Blend***)
8. We were willing to be open to unlimited potential of life and love again, without knowing how to do that, but just trusting. (sugg. Oils: ***Geranium, Bergamot, Encouraging Blend***)
9. We were willing to open ourselves to G.O.D. (sugg. Oils: ***Geranium, Calming Blend, Uplifting Blend***)
10. We continue to check in with ourselves, taking note if we became hateful toward ourselves or others, then, in an act of love, called for help in spite of our doubts, fears, or short-comings. (sugg. Oils: ***Black Pepper, Geranium, Lavender, Melissa, Cinnamon, Reassuring Blend***)
11. We committed to pray and meditate to improve conscious contact with Divinity, praying for the knowledge of its will for us and the strength to carry out our part. (sugg. Oils: ***Birch, Protective Blend, Roman chamomile, Ginger,*** add a ***Soul Support Collection Blend***)
12. We are having a spiritual awakening as a result of putting these steps into action, and continue the daily practice of love and acceptance in all our affairs.

APPENDIX 6 Returning Warriors Tearsheet

Returning Warriors *Hope with Oils Project*

VETERAN HEALTHCARE TODAY

is based largely on synthetic, patented medication.

- Companies design and patent
- FDA approves
- Doctors prescribe based on symptoms
- Patients consume

NATURE'S SOLUTIONS

FOR YOUR HEALTH

- Addresses root causes
- Very affordable, pennies per drop
- Available at home immediately
- No side effects vs. known/unknown side effects and addictions
- Used by ancient cultures for healthcare

He who has health, has hope; and he who has hope, has everything. - Thomas Carlyle

A desire to be in charge of our own lives, a need for control, is born in each of us. It is essential to our mental health, and our success, that we take control. - Robert Foster Bennett

WHAT ARE **ESSENTIAL OILS?**

- Extracts from plants
- Very Concentrated
- 50 to 70 times more powerful than herbs

THEY ARE 100% NATURAL

Make sure your oils are certified pure therapeutic grade oils

Similar health benefits to synthetic drugs **with NO Side Effects or Addictions**

- Addresses environmental and seasonal threats

Inside Threat

Cell

Outside Threat

Outer Membrane

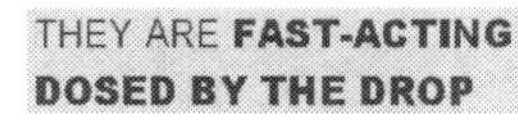

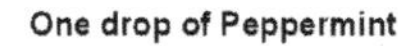

= **28 cups** of peppermint tea.

3 WAYS YOU CAN **USE ESSENTIAL OILS**

TOPICALLY

- Systemic, Localized effects
- Massage
- Immediate Comfort
- Immune Support

For those with sensitive skin or babies, always dilute with coconut oil for topical use

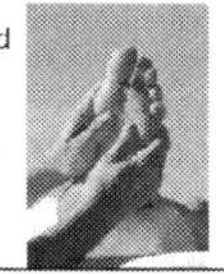

INTERNALLY

- Digestive System
- Mouth
- Throat
- Liver
- Urogenital Tract

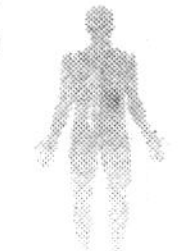

AROMATICALLY

- Affects Mood
- Cleanses Air
- Breathing Support

DISCLAIMER: The statements herein are provided for educational purposes only and are not meant to diagnose, prevent, cure, treat or heal disease, and have not been evaluated by the FDA. Professional medical care is always advised.

WARRIOR ESSENTIALS

VETIVER
Common Uses
- Supports healthy circulation
- Calming, grounding effect on emotions
- * Inhale for feelings of being triggered
- * Massage 1 drop on backs of hands
- * Use on brain stem
- * Inhale straight from bottle at onset of unsettling episode
- * Combine with Clove for enhanced soothing effect

OREGANO
Common Uses
- Used as a powerful cleansing & purifying agent
- Provides immune-enhancing benefits
- Supports healthy digestion & respiratory function
- Excellent source of antioxidants
- * Diffuse in carpeted areas for environmental threats
- * Use diluted with carrier oil on feet for environmental threats or occasional foot irritations

(**CAUTION:** possible drug interaction with diabetic medication, talk to your physician)

PEPPERMINT
Common Uses
- Promotes healthy respiratory function & clear breathing
- Alleviates occasional stomach upset
- Frequently used in toothpaste & chewing gum for oral health
- * Put 1 drop in glass of water & drink for occasional stomach upset due to nervous tension or food upset
- * Use topically 1 drop, massage on tired muscles associated with over exertion
- * Combine 2 drops each of Peppermint, Lemon & Lavender in glass of water & drink for seasonal threats

(**CAUTION:** may increase blood pressure, talk to your physician)

GROUNDING BLEND
Common Uses
- Calming, renewing fragrance
- Promotes relaxation & restful sleep
- Lessens tension, calms emotions, & helps reduce worry & stress
- Diffuses into a subtle aroma, ideal for aromatic benefits
- * Apply 2-3 drops on bottom of each foot in the morning
- * Inhale deeply. Use often during the day
- * Apply 1 drop under each armpit

DEEP SOOTHING BLEND PRODUCTS
Common Uses
- Comforts tired, sore joints & muscles
- Provides comforting sensation of cooling & warmth to problem areas
- Supports circulation to muscles & joints
- * Apply topically to affected areas
- * Take capsules as indicated

(**CAUTION:** Possible drug interaction with aspirin, Heparin, & Warfarin because wintergreen inhibits platelet adhesion & intensifies blood thinning, talk to your physician)

CLOVE
Common Uses
- Powerful antioxidant properties
- Promotes circulation
- Supports cardiovascular health
- Helps soothe teeth and gums
- Promotes oral health
- Supports a healthy immune system
- * Put 1 drop on finger and massage into back upper molars
- * Combine 1 drop each of Vetiver and Clove and massage on temples and back of neck for soothing effect
- * Use one drop in smoothies

(**CAUTION:** Very strong tasting in mouth but then numbing. Possible drug interactions with anti-depressants, Pethidine, serotonin re-uptake inhibitors, indirect sympathomimetic drugs. Talk with your physician)

LEMON
Common Uses
- Cleanses & purifies the air & surfaces
- Naturally cleanses the body & aids in digestion
- Supports healthy respiratory function
- Promotes a positive mood & cognitive ability
- Helps ward off free radicals with its antioxidant benefits
- Soothes an irritated throat
- * Use 2 drops lemon in glass drinking container with water several times a day (Do not use plastic containers)
- * Combine 2 drops each of Lemon, Lavender, & Peppermint in glass of water & drink 2x/day for seasonal threats
- * Diffuse in room to revive & freshen
- * Use 1 drop directly in throat for occasional discomfort

ESSENTIAL OIL CELLULAR COMPLEX
Common Uses
- Supports healthy cellular integrity by helping to reduce oxidative stress
- Supports healthy cellular function & metabolism
- Protects the body & cells from oxidative stress
- * Apply 2-3 drops topically over areas of concern
- * Take softgels as indicated

PROTECTIVE BLEND PRODUCTS
Common Uses
- Supports healthy immune function
- Protects against environmental threats
- Cleans surfaces
- Purifies skin while promoting healthy circulation
- Protective blend softgels also contain Melissa & Black Pepper
- * Use Protective Blend toothpaste to support gum & tooth health
- * Dilute in water & gargle in morning
- * Put 2 drops on bottom of each foot am & pm
- * Diffuse into air for cleansing
- * Take 5 drops in capsule 2x/day for alleviating environmental threats or use softgels

CILANTRO
Common Uses
- Rich in antioxidants
- Aids digestion
- Powerful cleanser and detoxifier
- Soothing to the skin
- Gives food a fresh and tasty flavor

EUCALYPTUS
Common Uses
- Assists with clear breathing
- Supports overall respiratory health
- Soothes tired, sore muscles
- Purifies and cleanses
- Helps to lessen stress
- Promotes oral health
- Supports healthy immune system function
- * Inhale when triggered from smell of sulphur, metal, ordinance
- * Combine 2 drops each of Eucalyptus & Helichrysum, massage around heart and cup hands over nose & inhale

LAVENDER
Common Uses
- Widely used for its calming & relaxing qualities
- Soothes occasional skin irritations
- Helps skin recover quickly
- Eases muscle tension
- * Diffuse in room
- * Apply topically undiluted to bottoms of feet at bedtime
- * Use in bathwater
- * Inhale straight from bottle
- * Massage around outer ear & earlobes for calming & relaxing
- * Keep at bedside and in glove box when driving

PROBIOTIC DEFENSE FORMULA
Common Uses
- Supports healthy digestive functions & immunities while creating an unfavorable environment for unhealthy elements
- Helps boost GI immunities
- Helps support optimal absorption of nutrients & energy metabolism
- Helps support healthy skin conditions
- Special double-encapsulation protects flora as they pass through the stomach
- * Take 1-3 capsules per day as indicated

DIGESTIVE BLEND PRODUCTS
Common Uses
- Aids in digestion
- Soothes occasional stomach upset or discomfort
- Supports a healthy gastrointestinal tract
- * Apply 1-2 drops topically to stomach area after meal
- * Put 2 drops under tongue
- * Use softgels for convenience or travel

(**CAUTION:** contains Peppermint which may increase blood pressure)

DISCLAIMER: These statements have not been evaluated by the FDA and are for informational purposes only. Always seek professional medical advice.

MELISSA
Common Uses
- Supports & helps boost a healthy immune system
- Calms tension & nerves
- Addresses occasional stomach discomfort
- Helps initiate a restful sleep
- Promotes emotional & cognitive health
- Uplifting lemony scent
- * Inhale deeply from bottle
- * Use products that contain it, like Protective Softgels, Joyful Blend, Respiratory drops to calm occasional fear due to uncommon life events

(**CAUTION:** Possible drug interaction with CYP2B6, talk to your physician)

BASIL
Common Uses
- Soothes sore muscles and joints
- Assists with clear breathing
- Acts a cooling agent for the skin
- Promotes mental alertness
- Lessens anxious feelings
- Enhances memory function
- Reduces stress and tension
- Soothes minor irritations
- Sharpens focus while studying or reading
- Soothes minor skin irritations
- * Use 2 drops in water 2x/day for tiredness due to occasional fatigue associated with temporary exhaustion
- * For ringing tones in ears associated with loud booms, apply 2 drops each of Basil & Frankincense & massage on outside of ears

RESPIRATORY BLEND PRODUCTS
Common Uses
- Maintains clear airways & breathing
- Supports overall respiratory health
- Calms the senses
- Supports mental clarity & function
- Helps minimize the effects of seasonal threats
- * Apply to chest, bottoms of feet, or backs of hands. Start with 1 drop
- * Inhale directly from bottle
- * Use for focused breathing exercises
- * Respiratory drops contain Melissa to help calm tension & nerves

FRANKINCENSE
Common Uses
- Helps build and maintain a healthy immune system
- Promotes cellular health
- Reduces the appearance of blemishes and rejuvenates skin
- Promotes feelings of peace, relaxation, satisfaction, and overall wellness
- * Inhale directly from bottle
- * 2 drops under tongue 3x/day as precaution
- * Apply to temples during times of fatigue or stress
- * Combine 1 drop each of Peppermint and Frankincense on hands, rub together and cup over nose for invigorating effect

HELICHRYSUM
Common Uses
- Helps skin recover quickly
- Promotes healthy liver function
- Supports localized blood flow
- Help detoxify the body
- Promote circulation
- Helps relieve tension
- * Apply 2 drops over heart daily for emotional work & support. Combine with 2 drops Eucalyptus for added effect
- * Massage around outside of ears for ringing tones & booming

BASIC VITALITY SUPPLEMENTS
Common Uses
- Food Nutrient Complex, Omega-3 fish oil, essential oils, & Cellular Vitality Complex support normal growth, function, and maintenance of cells
- Provides systemic benefits of vitality & wellness associated with optimal intake of essential nutrients
- Supports healthy metabolism & cellular energy
- Supports healthy immune function
- Supports bone health
- Enhances stamina and efficient use of oxygen
- Improves mental energy
- Helps to reduce the effects of fatigue and stress
- * Take 2x/day morning & evening or more as desired

To take control of your healthcare at home, please contact:

For scientific studies: **www.aromaticscience.com**

Reorder this tearsheet at **www.EssentialOilGear.com**

Get an Aroma Touch: **www.aromatouchtechnique.com**

APPENDIX 7 Oil Combinations

Lady Warrior Blend - Combine 2 drops ***Blend for Women*** (a pre-blended oil of ***Patchouli, Bergamot, Sandalwood, Rose, Jasmine, Cinnamon Bark, Cistus, Vetiver, Ylang-Ylang, Geranium, Cocoa Bean Extract, and Vanilla Bean extract)*** and 1 drop ***Joyful Blend*** for balancing and calming; smells wonderful!

Black Peppermint - Equal parts ***Black Pepper*** and ***Peppermint.***

Stinkfoot Powder - Use a cornstarch base, in a nice container, about a cup, and put 5 drops of one of the following oils:

For itchiness: ***Melaleuca*** or ***Eucalyptus***

For smell: ***Lavender, Frankincense***

For skin: ***Geranium, Myrrh***

For fungal: ***Arborvitae***

R.I.P. Blend - Equal parts ***White Fir*** and ***Calming Blend***! Very masculine.

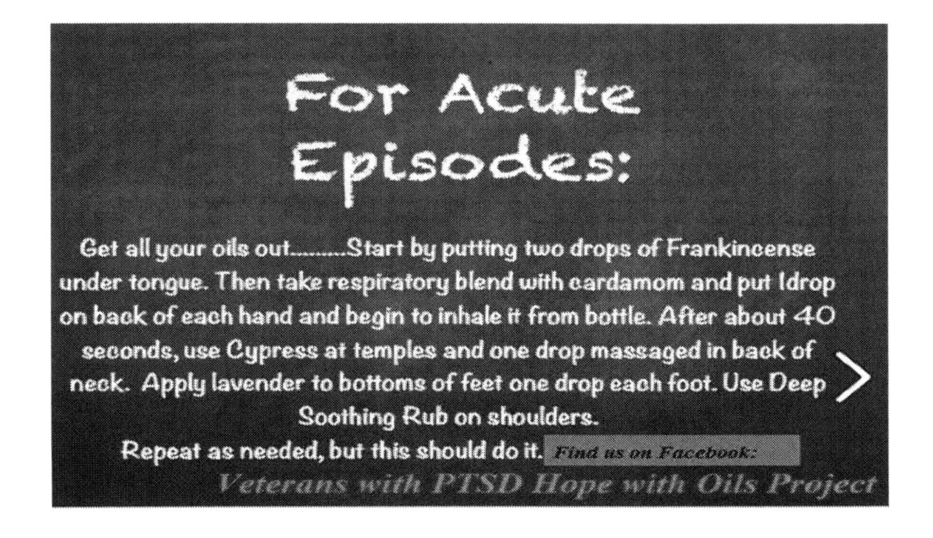

APPENDIX 8 References

http://aromaticscience.com for essential oil module learning

http://doterrablog.com/ for recipes and ideas

http://eft.mercola.com

www.pubmed.gov - to see studies, type "lavender oil anxiety" or any other oil in the search bar

JRDockers.com

Aromatouch Technique-A Clinical Approach to Essential Oil Application 2009)

https://www.facebook.com/pages/Veterans-with-PTSD-Hope-with-Oils-Project/

http://aromatools.com for supplies

cartoons courtesy of realwarriors.net

CONTACT your oils coach for complete listings of proprietary names of oils to order, usage, and tools, or contact oils4warriors@gmail.com.

NOTE: The statements shared in document have not been evaluated by the FDA. The products and methods recommended are not intended to diagnose, treat, cure or prevent any illness or disease, nor is it intended to replace proper medical help. Kindly understand that essential oils work to help bring the body into balance - thus helping the body's natural defenses restore homeostasis. Essential oils are not used to "treat" medical problems.

APPENDIX 9
LEADERS FAQ'S

A Perspective on Leadership

Many people ask where to start on this journey with veterans. Well, it's not hard, when darn near everyone we know has been a veteran, or is a veteran, or knows a veteran. I have only worked with veterans that are not currently serving. I am learning as I go. We don't have all the answers, but we started where we were at. Everyone has their own story on working with veterans and/or being a veteran working with veterans.

Everyone's idea on what a leader should look like, or how a leader should behave, or how to find one, is at best, subjective. There are as many leadership styles as there are humans. I'm just giving one perspective here as to what makes a good fit for helping veterans. To be a leader in sharing oils to veterans, it takes a certain kind of masochistic aspect to the personality, because you have to be able to withstand the avoidance pretty well, and be considered by others to perhaps be 'some kinda crazy' (at first anyhow), be rejected, be loving in spite of it all, be able to bounce back and learn from mistakes, be patient, and be happy to work for free more or less. You also have to have a belief that our veterans wrote a blank check to us for our freedoms with their lives, our government has largely forgotten them, and you are going to step up to the plate by sharing oils. That's what we do here. We help Vets with oils.

Sir Ernest Shackleton, an early 20th century explorer continues to inspire me and countless others, with the story of his intention to be the first man to cross the entire Antarctica. He needed a team to do it. He placed a recruitment advertisement in a newspaper for his famous Expedition that is legendary: It reads," MEN WANTED for hazardous journey, small wages, bitter cold, long months of compete darkness, constant danger, safe return doubtful, honor and recognition in case of success."

This ad proved to be catnip to masochistic adventurous men out there. They had what it took to join his trek to the South Pole.

I have often thought, that if Shackleton would have been looking for leaders to help Veterans with PTSD using oils, it would have said something like this:

Brave Souls Wanted

For healing journey, small wages, rejection,
long months of personal development,
constant uncertainty, large returns doubtful,
honor and recognition if successful.

The right people did turn out for the journey to sail with Shackleton. His ship was named Endurance, after his family motto: "With perseverance, we endure."

Unintentional events unfolded on that journey to cross the continent of Antarctica which was to show Shackleton's true leadership and character through the seemingly "impossible". His ship was slowly crushed by pack ice, leaving him and his men to survive on the ice. Stuff happened beyond all planning and intention. He did not give up, and promised to get all of his men back alive and did exactly that.

I continue to be inspired by such a man. We are on an adventure. We hope to offer health and healing to those "isolated in far away regions". We need not do this alone. We can join together, keeping in mind that there will be bumps along the way.

There are currently 450,000 veterans in need in various ways. We happen to offer oils for post-war stuff. And that's what we do. That is our "why".

Here are some things to consider that I have learned the hard way, that might help you. Call it an " Oils Manifesto".

#1 God is in charge. Over all of this. Prayer and giving it over are mindful acts we can do to not think we control things. We are not in control.

#2 For every good intention, there is the unintentional that can occur. This is where my growth happens, if I let it. I embrace the unintentional. I adjust. I reexamine. I adapt. (See #1.)

#3 I am enough. Right now. Just the way I am. I have what it takes.

#4 My intuition is always correct. I'm not afraid to follow it. Even if I screw up sometimes, it's ok.

#5 I don't need gimmicks to be motivated. I just need to know the truth of essential oils and 'why' I am doing them. The oils seem to have a life of their own. Once someone uses them, they understand. It's profound.

#6 It's ok to feel; to love; to screw up, to cry, to react. I am being human. I am growing all the time.

#7 If you are only sharing oils for the income you will be sadly disappointed and wasting your time. The income is lousy for the first 4 years.

#8 If you don't have a second income, or spouse support, or a fat trust fund, do not attempt to do this as a business. You should not try to do it on credit cards. Believe me.

#9 I can love and share oils. The rest is up to God.

#10 Beware of relying too heavily on aromatherapy tools, spending a lot on the latest thing, and getting into financial trouble doing it. This could cause undue pressure on marriage, pocketbook and other relationships. My best tool and asset is me. Showing up is the best thing. Putting a drop in someone's hand is best. I don't compare myself to others, or let myself feel "less than". I am enough. Buying the oils is paramount, ¼ dram sample bottles are helpful, business cards a must have, growth in essential oils knowledge, and a few other little things.

11 Social media is not human contact. Sometimes it's necessary to reach out using it, but I remember, humanity is best. I offer to do an oils class, or one-on-one session or a Wellness Consult. This is a big reason we encourage people to pick an Advocate from the Battle Buddy list because they will be IN CLOSE contact working with them; like the same city and state. We DISCOURAGE doing it "Club" style, thinking we can help from far distances, and trying to hit numbers and ranks. Certainly there is benefit to some degree, but

personal contact, therapy touches in person on a regular basis is best. We do not take advantage using our veterans.

#12 I am helping people; I contribute to their quality of life. I may from time to time gift an enrollment kit of oils if my intuition says to.

#13 I go to the person who enrolled me first, for suggestions if I get stuck.

#14 A lot of people hate doing anything on internet and refuse to. I find a way to reach them like phone or snail mail.

#15 I have felt like giving up more than once.

#16 I am curious and a life-long learner. I can learn from anybody, anywhere, anytime if I ask enough of the right questions.

#17 I am not a god. I can't fix anyone. I give all concerns to Him. I am just a fellow traveler with you on this Earth.

#18 Attitude is everything. I adjust mine, and release control. (See #1)

#19 Simplicity is my frame of reference. Simplifying and reducing are best.

#20 I understand my priorities. G-d, take care of self, family, then everyone else.

Q: How do I find Veterans to reach out to?

A: Vets are everywhere. Near bases is probably the easiest way to make connections. If you are teaching classes, make posters and hang in businesses that are frequented by soldiers on and off duty. (pray before going)

- ➔ Red Cross
- ➔ Military Spouses Groups
- ➔ Meet up groups online: meetup.com
- ➔ Friends and family
- ➔ Join the Facebook page: Veterans with PTSD Hope with Oils. You can request to be put on Battle Bud List as a contact. Many have gotten connected this way.

➔ Military Reunions

➔ Create a Facebook page

Q: Where can I find the Veterans Tearsheet to use in classes?

A: The tearsheet PDF for replication can be found here:

http://www.amazon.xom/PTSD-Veterans-Essential-Oil-Tearsheet

OR: to purchase tearsheets contact Oils4Warriors@gmail.com

Q: What do I say to a Veteran?

A: Say hello, and maybe ask where they served? If they are wearing a Viet Nam Vet ballcap I always walk up and say "Welcome Home." This always starts a lot of conversation. During the conversation, ask if they would be interested in trying a natural solution you know of for PTSD. Make sure you have some so you can give them a drop, and your business card. Always ask or have them smell it first before putting it on! Some vets will not want to try natural stuff, and that's ok.

Q: How do I get samples to a warrior?

A: Sending samples through the mail is easy, or handing them in person is good. Make sure to include a note detailing instructions on how to use. Include a business card. Ask for their number so you can call, but don't be surprised if you are turned down. Be patient. There are no guarantees here. This is not "business as usual". You are a very special Advocate if you are willing to work with Vets. Veterans can be reclusive and hyper-vigilant, and you are no exception.

Q: How long do I wait before following up?

A: Wait about a week. Call and see if the oil is being used. Ask if they like it.

Q: I'm certified with my massage table. How do I offer this?

A: As your relationship develops with troops, you can offer this service. Be sure it is on your business card!

Q: For quantity order discounts of this book, where can I go?

A: Contact the publisher at Oils4Warriors@gmail.com

Please allow 2-3 weeks for delivery for quantity orders.

****

Working with warriors can be a lot like “herding cats”...it is not going to be like you hope sometimes. Every bit of respect and patience will be needed to work in this realm. Be a learner. Be patient. For many vets it is really hard to reach out, or call back, or make decisions. Be ready, but not pushy or intrusive.

This is no easy task, and we know it. You are one of-a-kind doing this for vets, thank you!

63682611R00071

Made in the USA
Middletown, DE
03 February 2018